BECAUSE I SAID SO

CELINE SPARKS
FOREWORD BY JANIE CRAUN

Publishing Designs, Inc.
Huntsville, Alabama

Publishing Designs, Inc.
P.O. Box 3241
Huntsville, Alabama 35810

Cover art by Phyllis Alexander
Second Printing, February 2012

Printed in the United States of America

Publisher's Cataloging-in-Publication Data

Sparks, Celine, 1964—
Because I Said So / Celine Sparks.
Thirteen chapters.
1. Women—Christian Life. 2. Humor 3. Mother's sayings.
I. Title.
ISBN 978-0-929540-75-7
248.8

DEDICATION

To Daddy—
Who makes me laugh and helps me live,
and remembers it all when she said so.

Johnnie was Precious to me

ENDORSEMENTS

You are sure to laugh, you might even cry a little, when you read what "Mama said" in Celine Sparks' new book *Because I Said So*. Celine presents the Lord's way to live in a firm but humorous way. Be prepared; you won't be able to lay it down until you have finished reading it.

 —**Mack Lyon,** *In Search of the Lord's Way* Television Program

As you fly through this easy read you'll laugh out loud, you'll shed a tear, and you'll probably agree and nod passionately! You might even disagree a few times. But you're bound to hear the voice of a teacher who has a heart of compassion. Celine was obviously taught by a master teacher, her mom, who through simple godly wisdom gave her, and now gives us, a degree worth much more than one you'd hang you your wall. You will love this book! It is on my top ten list! You'll want to share this book with someone else . . . but . . . "Let Margie get her some first!" And Celine, good luck on that skydiving thing! Did I mention that you'll laugh?

 —**Dale Jenkins,** *A Minister's Heart*

Because I Said So is overflowing with marvelous applications of God's word seasoned with "down home" humor. Thank God for Celine's mama and for any mama who fearlessly stands on the Truth, lives the Truth, and teaches the Truth. As we say in the South, "Keep on a-writin', Celine, and tellin' it like it is!"

 —**Becky Blackmon,** *The Begging Place*

I love this book! A tribute to my mama and wise mamas everywhere, but most of all, an exposé of real wisdom that comes from the Good Book! It's a read I just couldn't rush, but then I found it difficult to put down. As I turned the pages, I reflected, repented, and resolved to be more the woman my great mother would want me to be. This book is a perfect solo study for women who want Christ to be real throughout their days. But dig deep into the scriptures presented and you have a practical ladies' class study book. Get your Bible when you read it, because you don't want to "go hunting without your gun!"

 —**Cindy Colley,** *Women of Troubled Times*, and other books

In today's society of gloom, doom, and discouragement, it is very encouraging to study ageless Bible principles in such a humorous and straight-forward way.
—**Lois Duncan Lyon,** Ladies' Lecturer

Having spent six years in medical school I never found "the funny bone" in my medical training. But I found it quickly within the pages of *Because I Said So*. However, my anatomy lesson did not end there. Celine Sparks points out the importance of possessing a sincere Christian backbone and actually doing something. With each new page you will find wit and wisdom, as she examines the Christian heart, the stomach (we can't have our cake and eat it too!), and our tongues. Never before in any study of anatomy did I laugh so hard—but those anatomy books never echoed the familiar phrases I had heard from my own mother! I found myself constantly pulling my wife over to read yet another delightful nugget of truth. Thanks Celine, for helping round out my medical education and dissecting my funny bone!
—**Brad Harrub, Ph.D.,** Executive Director, Focus Press, Inc

Celine never ceases to amaze me with her ability to make us laugh. Few are so gifted. In *Because I Said So*, Celine's charming wit grabs you and her Bible teaching convicts you. Without reservation, I recommend it for ladies' classes as well as personal use.
—**Jane McWhorter,** *Roses in December* and other books

Celine Sparks writes with a unique talent; she uses humor to teach. In this, her first book, Celine has produced a rich study that is easy to read.
—**Janie Craun,** *Heirlooms*, Editor *Christian Woman* magazine

Because I Said So is a book for women of all ages. It reminds us of what is most important in this life.
—**Rosemary McKnight,** *Those Who Wait* and other books

CONTENTS

FOREWORD

Did Jesus ever laugh? We know He was compassionate—He wept at a friend's funeral. But who can imagine the wedding feast at Cana without thinking that laughter was a part of that day's event? Or who pictures Him sharing time with close friends where no one ever said anything hilariously funny? It is hard to imagine that Jesus didn't have a sense of humor. His parables reveal him as a man of dry wit who often gained people's attention with an amusing remark before driving home some serious point to be remembered. It is a technique others have used with success, though none as skillfully as our Lord.

Celine Sparks writes with a unique talent; she uses humor to teach. I became a fan of Celine's several years ago when we began running many of her columns in *Christian Woman* magazine. Finding one of her submissions in the mail always made my day, and her articles never failed to give me a lift. With every chuckle was a nugget of solid instruction.

In this, her first book, Celine has produced a rich study that is easy to read. Those of my generation probably remember lots of "old sayings" our moms recited to us as we were growing up. You may recognize some of them here. Little did we realize then how instructive these gems of wisdom really can be!

I appreciate, especially, the straightforward manner in which the book addresses issues that we once discussed and debated, but too often we are neglecting to talk about today. The book is meaty, and hopefully it will lead us to rethink some behaviors that are becoming too commonplace in the Lord's body.

Elton Trueblood once observed that the Christian's well-known humor is not a way of denying the tears, but rather a way of affirming something deeper than tears. So Solomon was absolutely right when he observed that "there is a time to weep, and a time to laugh" (Ecclesiastes 3:4). This book may cause you to do both. Read and enjoy.

—*Janie Craun*

INTRODUCTION

Words that Stick

All mamas are ordinary, and yet not one of them is. They can say things that don't make a bit of sense, and yet somehow send a message that bypasses the entire nervous system and penetrates the core of your soul. It's a gift, a benefit that comes with the position.

There are hundreds of these little sayings in an unwritten manual, and no matter how much you determine that when you get to be a mother you're not going to use them, you'll find that it's as hard to separate motherhood from these phrases as Kool-Aid from a couch.

I imagine Eve herself must have strolled through the garden listing what she wanted done "this very minute" or else she was going to "tan some hides." I imagine even the camel got tired of hearing "Don't make me pull this thing over." When frustrated, she was probably very gifted at spitting the things they had just said back at the boys, such as when Abel said, "I'm just going over here to sharpen this arrow," she said, "I'll sharpen *your* arrow!" And I picture after sin made havoc of her home in a way that only sin can, she hung her head as Cain headed out of the tent door for Nod, and as teardrops splashed on her leopard skin, she quietly said, "Call me when you get there."

These little things mamas say stick with us for a lifetime, maybe because of the importance of who said them, maybe because of our keen memory at the time they were first spoken to us — whatever the reason, the words live forever.

That's why I needed the help of Mama's words to write this book. I have no words that live forever. Mamas don't really have them either I guess. There is only one Source for words that live forever (Matthew 24:35).

Echoes from *The Book*

It's just that those "mama" expressions are but echoes of harder, firmer and more valuable truths, and I think that's the reason they stick. "Can't never could" is just a maternal twist on Philippians 4:13, and "Pretty is, as pretty does" is a mama's translation of Proverbs 31:30, only easier to memorize.

That's why I employ these idioms—they're easy to memorize. In fact, for the most part, we already have. We had no choice about it. Now let's apply them. That's where the book comes in.

Some of the chapter titles you'll recognize immediately, and will probably take you back to all the scents and décor of an avocado den or a dinged up station wagon—wherever it is that your mother hovered over you or cradled you close. Others of them are unique to my mama, because while mothers share universal concerns like making sure your underwear has no holes in it because if you have a serious wreck, you would not want to be embarrassed in front of the emergency room staff, each also has her own repertoire of verbal standbys, which only make sense within the family, and which are handed down like china and Confederate coins.

I could write a second volume inspired by my mother-in-law containing chapter titles like "Quit Acting Like an Afegucius," "Tell It, Ellen" and "The Maid Didn't Come," but I simply entered the picture too late, and so I sometimes have a glazed look at the family gatherings.

But even in those made-from-scratch sayings (which compose eight of the thirteen chapter titles), we can pull out a code for living. That's what mamas do—they give us a code for living, or at least they should.

Unfolding Truth in a Spoonful of Sugar

Within each chapter, I have tried to focus on the scriptural unfolding of a biblical truth. I have treated this study as carefully as measuring medicine into a dropper, but as Mary Poppins always told us, it goes down a lot easier with a spoonful of sugar.

And so, after each chapter, you will find a section called *Spark Plugs*. It is there for no other reason than to help the medicine go down. You can skip over it if you like. It will not give you spiritual insight or practical wisdom, but I suspect if you're striving for either of those, it might give you something you need along the way.

These are just humor columns, so don't try to get anything out of them. They will not fill your bucket; they will just make it more fun to carry.

I once went to church with a man who thought it was a sin to laugh during Bible class. He must have some distant relatives all over the United States who occasionally write or email me about my published humor columns to let me know that they don't get it, they don't appreciate that most other people do get it, and that their funny bone has been broken since the third grade or has been surgically removed.

I wouldn't want to be around when their commode stops up or they brown the casserole too long. Sometimes it's good to laugh; I'd even say it's vital. It won't get us to heaven, but it will help us over some of the hurdles which, otherwise, can keep us from trying.

Sometimes someone will say to me, "I always read your column first." I'm amazed, that in a magazine chockfull of excellent treatises on critical issues surrounding us, our families, and the church, that they can't flip over to the frivolous fast enough. It speaks volumes.

We spend the month immersed in the important which is usually upstaged by the urgent. How is it that we cope? Scripture, prayers, and occasionally a long row of Z's. But there's another built in mechanism, sometimes involuntary, that our Designer put there to release tension, to refresh our spirit and to help us with perspective and perseverance. We are the only created beings with the ability to laugh. What a shame if we disregard such a blessing! So go ahead, read it first when that month's magazine comes, snort out loud and fall over in your salad if you want to. It's not that I'm particularly funnier than the next person; it's just that you may already be overdue for a good case of the giggles, or else you're going to need it before you round life's next corner.

After you bray a little, you can get past the appetizers to the real sustenance. I hope each of us can find some within these pages. This book was written with you in mind and in prayers, my Christian sisters who remind me of the cast of *The Muppet Show*. We come in all shapes and shades, and have but one thread that binds us all together. It is the only thread that matters.

For My Heroes

At times, this book may seem to speak more directly to one strain of us than the others. Sometimes it is the married, or the older, or those with children at home. Please bear with me if any one chapter is not sensitive to your unique circumstances. You are all my heroes – the divorced, the single, and those hitting golden anniversaries, those in the third world and those in my back yard, those with vans cluttered up with tennis balls, hula hoops and transformers, and those staring at four walls of framed memories – this book is for you.

I don't pretend to understand your individual struggles or strengths, but when I was working on *Because I said So*, I made it a point to stay in touch with Someone who does. When the publisher first approached me about this project, I thought, *Why me? I'm nothing but a sinner bought with blood.* I guess those last three words made me reconsider, and in the words of Mama in the first chapter, I guess I decided to . . .

Do *something* if I have to repent of it.

You decide.

Top: Johnnia Duncan, age 8.

Middle: Johnnia holding Celine, 1965.

Bottom: Celine and her fourth child Enoch, 2003.

CHAPTER 1

DO SOMETHING, IF YOU HAVE TO REPENT OF IT!

Christianity Undone

If ye know these things, happy are ye if ye do them.
—John 13:17 KJV

My cousin Deana was sitting on the step to the washhouse. (I never knew it was a utility room until I went to college.) I was on the toy box whose lid was barely shut because things like jumper cables and souvenir sunglasses were trying to emerge from it.

"I don't know. What do you want to do?" It was a dangerous question to ask the cousin who once used concrete and a socket wrench to see if CorningWare really was unbreakable. The bike tires were flat, the swimming pool had become a test lab for tadpoles, and I didn't dare suggest hide-n-seek. Deana didn't like to count, and when she hid, she was really, really good. I knew I wouldn't see her again until Christmas.

We kept our voices low because if Mama found out we were looking for something to do, she would accommodate us, and it might include vinegar, Murphy soap, and baseboards. One of our nicknames for Mama, though, was "Bionic Ears." It's amazing that she could hear the minutest detail of a phone conversation—both ends!—with a boyfriend, from another room of the house when the vacuum was running and a train was passing.

True to her nickname, she cracked the screen door, looked at Deana and me, and said, "Well, do something if you have to repent of it."

• •

That was neither the first nor the last time Mother used the phrase, and it stuck hard not only to me but my brother and sisters as well. We say it to our kids, and occasionally it will come out of my mouth at a ladies' meeting or a teen planning session.

But do I really want my kids or any Christian to do something they will have to repent of? Absolutely not! Did Jesus really want the church at Laodicea to be cold? (Revelation 3:15). Should we really continue in sin that grace may abound? (Romans 6:1). Is it really a great thing to have a millstone tied around your neck, and be thrown in the ocean? (Mark 9:42). Of course not! Read the whole verse. Hear the whole idiom. The emphasis in Mama's statement lies in the first half: *Do something*. What follows her "if" only emphasizes it all the more.

Perhaps she didn't phrase it quite as eloquently as Edmund Burke in his famous quotation, "All that is necessary for evil to succeed is that good men do nothing," but she was right on the money.

The Easiest Choice

The choice to do nothing is popular because it is frankly the easiest choice to make. In fact, we're unaware that we've even made a decision at all. It wins by default. If we "sit on the step of our washhouse" long enough, the devil can have a hey-day destroying every life in his path, and it will be no one's fault in particular. It's like a bill sitting on the President's desk. Doing nothing is the same as signing it into law.

What if a medical doctor worked that way? What if he merely wondered if he should do something about a malignant tumor but was unsure of the best route and merely delayed any course of action until, until . . . well he's really not sure, but at least until later? What if firefighters worked that way? Or soldiers? What if the best plan of strategy in a war seemed to be simply to do nothing?

As Christians, we are armed soldiers (Ephesians 6:11). The emergency at hand is more critical than even a malignancy or a four-alarm fire. In spiritual matters, the consequences of doing nothing are eternal, as in forever and ever. It isn't that lives are at stake; it's that souls are at stake.

> *I must work the works of Him who sent Me while it is*
> *day; the night is coming when no one can work.*
>
> —John 9:4

The No-Risk Choice

It's a given that there are risks involved when we choose to do something about a situation because we know as Christians we should. Let's look at a couple of real-life examples.

Example One: Neglect of Abuse

When I was a young preacher's wife, I received an upsetting phone call. The lady on the other end was someone I looked up to very much, and yet she was asking advice from me. She had some orphaned children visiting in her home only for the weekend, and she highly suspected from what the children told her that there was abuse in the permanent foster home. I tossed and turned, I weighed and balanced, I prayed and walked the floor, but in the end, I'm so ashamed to say I did nothing. I hope the Lord will forgive me, and while I pray for these now grown children whom I have never seen again, it haunts me to know that my default decision may have impacted their life forever. I regret to say that there were risks involved. I knew who the foster parent was, and I could picture his brawny but burly physique threatening my own secure family if I reported him. I tried to find comfort by telling myself that I had no real evidence and that it was really the decision of the lady who phoned me.

Why couldn't I hear Mama's motto at that crucial time, "Do something if you have to repent of it!"?

Example Two: Poring and Pouring

Steven and Callie looked forward to a class reunion at a Christian school with great anticipation, because one of the highlights of the three-day event was Sunday worship on the school grounds. Another was a family day at a nearby church fellowship hall. It was the event between those two that was troubling. They arrived at the formal dinner to find classmates poring over old annuals and scrapbooks, but that wasn't all they were pouring. Each had a half-empty glass in his or her hand, a glass that held a martini, a margarita, red wine, white wine—the list is exhaustive except for milk and Kool-Aid. Most had been at the church gym earlier, and most would be at worship later.

Steven was convicted that the behavior was displeasing to his God who said, "Wine is a mocker, strong drink is raging, and whosoever is deceived thereby is not wise" (Proverbs 20:1 KJV). The choice was obvious; they would leave. As they rounded the corner, they ran into Kevin and Marley, and they began not only reflecting back, but looking forward together to brotherhood lectureships and upcoming spiritual events. And Steven and Callie couldn't help but notice, there were no drinks in Kevin or Marley's hand. The couples both opted to stay and be uplifted by one another – the four of them alone at a table for ten.

The "what ifs" usually intimidate and force people into doing absolutely nothing.

In the ensuing weeks, the scenario would not go away in Steven's mind—the friends he had swung from the monkey bars with in kindergarten, the girls who broke his heart in junior high, and the chemistry partners who almost blew up the lab together—they had all been at the reunion enticed by one of Satan's favorite lures, and in the words of Solomon, strongly deceived. Steven wondered if he should say or do something, but how could he risk friendships that meant so much to him? And besides, would anybody really listen? What if these people became angry?

The "what ifs" usually intimidate and force people into doing absolutely nothing. But not this time! Maybe Steven would take the wrong course or choose the wrong words, but failed attempts are always better than no attempt.

That's exactly what Mama said, isn't it? Do *something* if you have to repent of it. And that's a pretty big if, I might add.

Steven spent the next days agonizing over an email, making sure he expressed his love, but imploring his classmates to consider the scriptures, their personal influence, and the implications of their actions for their children's lives. In response, some bonds were strengthened, and some were distanced.

Five months later, one of the classmates he emailed was buried. What if Steven had ignored the "do something" plea from within?

Spiritual immobility usually brings regret, but conscience-stirred action rarely does!

Be Strong and Courageous

The risks you and I encounter every day, whether real or imaginary, can paralyze us, but this will not do because there are cities to conquer; there are walls to tear down. Are we really that far removed from our "pedestaled" hero, Joshua? Isn't it significant that when his task was laid out before him, God had to instruct him and remind him six times in one short chapter, "Only be strong and very courageous"? The wording of the phrase was the same all six times. Joshua was obviously an intelligent man, and yet God kept reinforcing this one concept. Not only was he intelligent, but his role was minimal: God was going to do all the conquering for him. The ratio remains the same in our work some thousands of years later. God does the conquering. You cannot fail. Only be strong and very courageous.

> *. . . and so I will go to the king, which is against the law; and if I perish, I perish.*
> —Esther 4:16

The Choice That Fits My Circumstances

The "something" in the phrase "do something" leaves us wide open to an array of choices that fit our talents. The "do nothing" mindset often walks in the door when we begin to wonder what we could do. The "I'm just one person," "someone else could do a better job," "that's not my talent" and other negative self-talk phrases that go through our head are straight from Satan, the father of lies (John 8:44).

Betty's Mama

Betty's mama was poor and uneducated. She never got a new do, and never sported the latest fashion, but she knew the truth in my own mama's statement. When a family in her neighborhood was dealing with unexpected death, she didn't have a freezer full of vegetables to prepare or even a pretty card to send, but she showed up with what she did have. Betty's mama entered the grieving home with an old rag and a can of shoe polish. She didn't have eloquent condolences to offer, but went straight to work. Opening the bedroom closets, she began to get each family member's dress shoes out, and with great care, shined each of them to near perfection. It was a chore the family could not even begin to be concerned about at the time, but one that would enable them to show respect to their loved one as the funeral hour approached.

Betty's mama could have listened to many inside voices arguing that her resources were too limited to help when she was needed, but instead, she listened to the one voice that said, "Do something." I'm sure many people offered a wealth of verbal condolences that day. I'm sure many glorious casseroles were arrayed and beautiful flower arrangements were delivered. I'm also sure that every single one of these casseroles, kind words, and flowers has faded from memory with the passing of time. But one act remains in vivid color, and its story is being passed down, all because Betty's mama chose to do something. It kind of reminds me of the lady in Mark 14 whose unique act of kindness was criticized. However, Jesus said it would be told as a memorial wherever the gospel was spread (Mark 14:9).

Our choices are unlimited in doing something. Galatians 6:10 says, "Therefore, as we have opportunity, let us do good to all." What is your opportunity, and what is your talent? Remember, it can be as humble as operating an old shoe rag.

From Linda's Chair

Linda's sense of humor can vaporize a tear midstream. A tough and loving disciplinarian to her three teens, she remains a pillar of support to her husband Scott, recently diagnosed with advanced cancer. Linda teaches classes, opens her home for service group meals, works late hours decorating for VBS and other activities, and is involved in every line of church work imagined, including secretary. I can get tired just thinking about it, and all of this is done from her wheelchair, though it is better known as a taxi for the toddlers who line up for rides. On at least two occasions, Linda has quickly pushed herself from her chair so that it might be used for another church member in an emergency situation.

Most of us could go on about someone with equal energy in challenging circumstances, but the lesson can be summed up in two words: do something! Yes, your resources might be more limited than someone else's; your talents may pale in comparison. But what about your opportunities? Without even knowing your name or where you live, I'd bet my last dollar—if I were a bettor—that your opportunities abound! It's not hard to find an opportunity to do good; it's hard to find someone to grab hold of the opportunity.

> *There is a lad here who has five barley loaves and two*
> *small fish, but what are they among so many?*
> —John 6:9

Satan's Time—Later!

We've already established that Satan is the father of lies. While we most commonly characterize him as the vicious dictator making men and women commit murder, adultery, armed robbery, kidnapping, and other violent acts, we don't give him enough credit for his "behind-the-scenes" work. He doesn't want any credit. He'd rather sit quietly and whisper to "good" men and women that they are doing enough already. He's quite effective at convincing us that the perfect time to get involved is later, the best person for the job is a talented brother or sister, and the best method of evangelism is silence until it "comes up."

When you or I have an opportunity to do something, which is constantly, and we shift our feet and look around until the opportunity is passed, the feet that are shifting are those in Pilate's sandals. Pilate had the opportunity to free the innocent. He knew what he should do; there's no doubt about that, but the wheels began turning in his head. He began to visualize those risks associated with being no friend of Caesar's. He took his wife's advice and chose to "have nothing to do with that just man" (Matthew 27:19).

It was "doing nothing" that crucified my Savior. You don't have to actively choose to sin in order to crucify him afresh.

"To him who knows to do good, and does not do it, to him it is sin" (James 4:17). Even Mama couldn't make it any plainer than that.

Do something, or you *will* have to repent of it!

> *To him who knows to do good,*
> *and does not do it, to him it is sin.*
>
> —James 4:17

Something for <u>YOU</u> to Do . . .

1. Think about your own experiences. What do you view as the most common risks that we associate with jumping into a situation, and doing something about it?

2. In the scenario concerning Christians drinking at a social event, do you think another course of action would have been better? Reflect on times when you have been put in that same situation.

3. What specific lies has Satan used to convince you of your ineffectiveness?

4. Discuss Pilate's predicament. Make a list with two columns, the first with the consequences Pilate considered if he freed Jesus; the second with the consequences Pilate considered if he crucified Jesus.

Pilate's Consequences

Do It   Don't Do It

5. Now use the chart you just made to evaluate your own choices concerning a specific challenging situation you face. Are any of the consequences you perceive the same as those Pilate considered?

My Consequences

Do It   Don't Do It

～ Spark Plugs ～

And speaking of high school reunions . . .

I think the last time I got all my children and their father around the actual dinner table at the same exact time was in 2003, and that was because we had received mail from Auburn football coach Tommy Tuberville. Unfortunately, there was no food. Now before you write me up in your church bulletin and declare me an official unfit mother, let me explain that we often do have dinner (or at least Hot Pockets) around a table set for six. I use the term "set" of course loosely because I learned from Mama that the most efficient way to "set" a table is to open the silverware drawer, grab a handful of forks, and place the pile next to the centerpiece (spare bike part). It's not that we don't make an effort to have the family gathered around the dinner table; it's just that one of our chair legs is missing the thingy on the bottom that equalizes it with it's other three legs and so no one wants to sit in that chair, and so we sit at the other five in turns as a sort of unstructured game of musical chairs without the music (though we do have a strong vocals and percussion section).

It works like this: Person one gets up to get the milk. Person six sits in person one's chair. Four grabs a towel to clean spilled milk; one sits in four's chair; three takes the towel to the laundry room; four sits in three's chair; two realizes milk is still out and believes she'll have a refill; six hops up to scrape peas in garbage can while two isn't looking; two grabs six's chair; six goes to find three who forgot where the laundry room is; one licks four's fork and has to get him a new one. Three reenters with dirty towel, takes one's chair; two goes to find six who forgot who he was trying to find. Four runs to bedroom to make it in time for final Jeopardy. Three gets up to answer the phone and says, "Yes, I don't think we have credit card debt, but I have a kitten." One realizes he is the only one left to do the dishes, and has acute appendicitis.

So my point is, if I can't get six people who are confined to one house around a table for three minutes, who can imagine that they can get fifty-six people scattered all over the U.S. and Puerto Rico to one central location for a high school reunion? It's a preposterous idea, and yet people keep trying it. There are many common reasons people can't attend their high school reunions. Many simply live too far, many have business trips or vacations scheduled in conflict, some have illnesses, but by far, the number one reason that people miss their high school reunions is that they are too fat.

Some people actually try to overcome this hurdle by fasting for two weeks before the event. For some reason, it is really important to these people to be able to tuck their shirt in and zip their pants. They imagine, I guess, that other people will not be able to zip their pants and will be walking around with an un-tucked, long flowing shirt which everyone will mistake for a maternity top. These people will be pointing and quietly whispering, "Look at Michelle; she can still zip her pants."

The irony in this is that in high school, our teachers told us with a straight face that we would really need to know the abbreviations for all the elements in the periodic table to succeed in life. It turns out twenty years later, all that really matters is if you're able to zip your pants. It's the only revenge we have left. No longer can we buy out the cheap toilet paper company and go rolling after midnight. No putting stink bombs in lockers or tying shoestrings to desk chairs. Those days are gone forever. They were the unmistakable message of disapproval at switching girlfriends mid-choral concert or getting a perfect score on the chemistry exam, thus eliminating all hope for a curve.

Now we walk by with zipped pants as a subtle way of saying, "You could have asked *me*! I *wanted* to go to the Beta banquet! Now look at me. I'm happily married, have four kids, a big screen TV, and I can zip my pants! Whaddaya say to *that*?"

Of course the conversation goes much more like this:

"So where are you living now?" (Translation: I don't remember you at all.)

"New Hope." (New Hope.)

"Is that the new subdivision up on the mountain?" (Okay, just any indication at all of who you might be?)

> No longer can we buy cheap toilet paper and go rolling after midnight.

"Yeah, it popped up about ten years ago." (I used to have hair. You do remember that I used to have hair, right?)

"It's nice. I've got a friend that looked at a lot out there." (Wait a minute! You used to have hair.)

"We enjoy it. It's got a nine-hole golf course."(You're looking at my bald head again. What is it with this class?)

"Really? We'll have to get together sometime."(It's Scott I think. Or James. Oh, which is it?)

"Okay, great! Give me a call sometime when you're in town." (Your mother made Rice Krispy squares for the bake sale. Is she alive?)

The only thing worse than flitting around from conversation to conversation is being the spouse of the flitter. This is when you actually say out loud that you don't remember anyone or have any funny stories to share.

At my husband's reunion recently—this is absolutely true—I listened to an in depth argument for some twenty-three-and-a-half minutes about who was in the red group and who was in the blue group. I'm still uncertain, but one of these groups went on a field trip to the post office wherein the teacher instructed everyone to bring eight cents for a stamp (roars of laughter). And of all things, there were live chickens at the post office that day. I fished in my husband's pocket for the car key and went to a yard sale nearby to kill time. No one missed me.

Wait a minute! You used to have hair.

"I'm famished," Michelle says with her pants zipped.

"Oh, I can tell," the rest of us murmur inside, "by the way you've picked at your parsley."

It's a tormenting evening because not one woman wants to be the only one to clean her plate. And yet there is this gnawing reminder inside that this one plate cost seventy dollars, this month's payment on the big screen TV. And a truffle is a terrible thing to waste.

Then it's about to happen. The class president stands from her table. It's awards time. Oh please no. Wasn't this embarrassing enough the first time? Didn't I know I was most likely to drop my books on the bus steps without everyone voting?

Everyone is giggling in anticipation as if the half-truffle-left-on-plate thing isn't bothering them anymore. We applaud for the person who drove the farthest, is married the longest, has the most children, and what?—the first grandmother? When did that happen? How old are we?

There are lots of congratulations and pictures, but somehow a blanket of discomfort has fallen over the group. It's as if everyone is secretly consumed with this grandmother thing. Grandmother, as in the person who makes you laugh by taking out her teeth?

My thoughts are interrupted as Michelle squeezes between my husband and me on the way out the door, and says out loud, "That's not a maternity top, is it?" She winks, and is gone.

"You have any cash?" I ask my husband, "I'd like to buy out the cheap toilet paper company on the way home."

Johnnia Duncan,
early teaching
years, 1950s.

Top: Young Johnnia, age 8, with girl dog "Ted."

Middle: Lee Holder with Johnnia Duncan Holder and her mother Mattie "Dunca" Duncan.

Bottom: Johnnia with third child Sami.

CHAPTER 2

...AND WELL WORTH IT!

The Hidden Cost of Sin

As a bird hastens to the snare,
He did not know it would cost his life.

—Proverbs 7:23

It seemed that everything in the toy department was too expensive. Plus, I always received the answer, "You don't need that." Of course I didn't need it! Toys do not supply food or shelter, but I wanted it. So I would scrounge around the store until I finally found something I thought was cheap enough.

"Look, Mom, it's a little pink man with a piece of plastic wrap and a lot of little strings all tangled up."

"It's a parachuter," the scholar sibling answered.

"But it's a nickel, Mom. That's not much. It's a nickel."

She examined him over her glasses, "And well worth it."

• •

"And well worth it" was Mama's way of saying, "You get what you pay for." She had seen the pink parachuters before. They promise a few minutes of fun, but they don't parachute at all. They fall. The string is wrapped around the soldier's neck in one place and the support has come loose from his back at another. There is a mass of string to untangle, and the project is soon deserted. Even the dog finds it a disappointing chew, getting more dental floss than he had bargained for.

Growing up, I found out that "the well worth it" department didn't just consist of the toy aisle. The world has a host of cheap promises.

A Few Minutes of Fun

Many a life has been destroyed for a few minutes of fun. I can't think of a better example of the lifelong consequences of one short round of fun than David's bout with Bathsheba. Or what about Herod, who asked his stepdaughter to dance for his friends, and got so caught up in the few minutes of fun that he promised her half his kingdom? (Matthew 14). She opted, instead, for the head of John the Baptist. Judah saw a prostitute by the side of the road. Not even having the money on him, the few minutes of fun he could enjoy were so tempting, he got her with an IOU and a "please." He was traveling, no one would know, and yet it ended in humiliation and incestuous pregnancy (Genesis 38).

We see the same results on the news in the lives of politicians, and we are all too familiar with results that are closer to home. A few minutes of sin are never concluded in the few minutes. "Then, when desire has conceived, it gives birth to sin; and sin, when it is full-grown, brings forth death" (James 1:15).

"You're About to Fall!"

A parachuter was meant to soar. The descent is the closest thing to flying we wingless creatures can feel. But the end of the cheap plastic pink parachuter is not a soar at all, but a fall. Again we find the nickel spent to be "well worth it."

In addition to Mama's way with words, she had another quality we remember with laughter. My mama fell *all the time*. And I don't mean when she was elderly—she lived to be only 62. My mama fell at church, at the mall, at work, at home, downtown, and on picnics. She should have been a stunt woman. If you're going to fall anyway, you may as well get paid for it.

Walking with Mama, I pointed out "wet floor" signs; I pointed out uneven lay of the tile; I reminded her of every door's threshold and quickly kicked outdoor obstacles out of the way. These were big warning signs: "You're about to fall!" Mama, by and large, ignored them, and we had another good "fall story" and a few more stitches.

The Bible is heavy on yellow cones of warning. "You're about to fall," they communicate, and yet we continue to ignore them for the few minutes of fun we're anticipating. Here are some of them:

Steadfastness begins to crumble. "You therefore, beloved, since you know this beforehand, beware lest you also fall from your own steadfastness, being led away with the error of the wicked" (2 Peter 3:17). Peter's readers are steadfast. This is your Wednesday night crowd. Yet Peter sees a danger. There is a constant danger to the faithful of being led away with error. We have seen it happen over and over. The person who used to believe and teach and even preach the truth has now compromised it. How did it happen? Back up a verse. Verse 16 talks about unstable people who twist the Scriptures to their own destruction. These people have fallen not because they listened to pop psychologists or went into worldly places. They were led away by listening to people discussing Scriptures, people who were twisting those Scriptures into error instead of accepting them as the truth. Peter puts up a yellow cone here. If someone is putting a "new twist" on an established truth, you may be listening to error. Beware, Peter says, it could be that you're about to fall.

Integrity begins to waver. "But above all, my brethren, do not swear, either by heaven or by earth or with any other oath. But let your 'Yes,' be 'Yes,' and your 'No,' 'No,' lest you fall into judgment" (James 5:12). Can people be confident that something is true if I'm the one who said it? Is my yes really yes, or is it maybe? Is my no really no, or is it "I don't remember"?

If my word is good, there is never any need to say, "I swear to you," or "So help me, if this is not true, I'll—" Those are the words of a person who lacks integrity. They say, "This time, I really am telling the truth."

Examine your dialogue. What is the real cause of uncertainty in answers? If half-truths and misleading words are emerging, be careful. James says you're falling.

> *But above all, my brethren, do not swear, either by heaven*
> *or by earth or with any other oath. But let your "Yes," be*
> *"Yes," and your "No," "No," lest you fall into judgment.*
>
> —James 5:12

⊕ *Materialism starts battling for first place.* "But those who desire to be rich fall into temptation, into a snare, into many senseless and harmful desires that plunge people into ruin and destruction" (1 Timothy 6:9 ESV). This verse does not say that rich people fall; it says that people who want to be rich fall. Would I be in that category? Am I after senseless desires? It is told that Elvis got into his private jet one night and flew to Denver, Colorado, in pursuit of a peanut butter, jelly, and bacon sandwich. Is that a senseless desire? It wasn't to Elvis. Are you and I so consumed with the pursuit of material things that our Maker would call it senseless? But the people we see who can do the things we would like to do, and have the things we would like to have are not plunged into ruin and destruction, are they? They're on top of the world, the top of the charts, and how we wish we could trade places with them! Hold it! Do we? Elvis died of an overdose, and awaits eternal judgment. How many of the rich and famous are in line for the gates of heaven? The ruin and destruction 1 Timothy 6:9 addresses are not bankruptcy and foreclosure. There is a danger of ruining our chance of heaven and facing everlasting destruction because we were pulled away by a senseless desire. Are you falling?

Cheap Shoes

The New Testament provides other yellow "fall" cones:

⊕ pride (1 Timothy 3:6)

⊕ bitterness (Hebrews 12:15)

⊕ disobedience (Hebrews 4:11)

⊕ self-righteousness (1 Corinthians 10:12)

⊕ spiritual shallowness (Luke 8:13)

These are not just your average smoking, drinking, and sleeping around categories. Sin is easy, and she will present herself in the shoes that fit, wherever your feet happen to be standing at the time. In the end, these are the shoes that cause the fall. Cheap shoes, and "well worth it."

The String Is Wrapped Around the Soldier's Neck

Sin is easy, but recovery from the fall is not. Ask an A. A. member how easy recovery is. Ask the woman carrying the baby conceived with an intern at lunch. Ask those whose DUI charges have escalated to manslaughter. Suddenly there is a string entangled in complicated knots. Sin in her pretty pink package has laid her trap, and the string is wrapped around the neck of her prey. I have sat across the table from a few of the entangled, and I have been in that chair myself, and the words are always similar, "I knew it was wrong, but I never thought it would turn out like this."

The Support Has Come Loose

Finding ourselves in the midst of sin's ruin, helplessness is multiplied by spiritual loneliness. It happened to the prodigal son in Luke 15. After the yellow cones were ignored, after the fall, after the entanglements had taken his money and his dignity, he found himself alone in the filth and mire of pigs and their refuse. He had walked away from his family. He had walked away from his father. The support had come loose from his own doing, and he found himself in a place where he needed it most.

The shelter and security of God's love and protection are the greatest blessings a Christian can experience this side of death. This is a support that carries us in the times when we simply cannot carry ourselves. Psalm 121 gives us a grasp of the all-encompassing nature of His care. The magnitude of the loss of this support is devastating.

He has promised never to leave us or forsake us (Hebrews 13:5), and that if we will come near to Him, He will be near to us (James 4:8). Life's storms cannot hit hard enough to shake loose the bond. "For I am persuaded that neither death nor life, nor angels nor principalities nor powers, nor things present nor things to come, nor height nor depth, nor any other created thing, shall be able to separate us from the love of God which is in Christ Jesus our Lord" (Romans 8:38–39).

There is only one barrier that can separate us from God, and it is one that we choose to put in place. "Your iniquities have separated you from your God; and your sins have hidden His face from you" (Isaiah 59:2).

It's the hard truth: sin separates.

The Project Is Soon Deserted

When sin is through, and she has separated you from that which matters most, the project is deserted. Sin plans big, and then burns the plans. No doubt, Ananias and Sapphira had big plans for the proceeds from their money deal (Acts 5). They could picture themselves quite the church and community leaders . . . sin's big plans. I wonder just what Gehazi's plans were with his newly acquired wardrobe (2 Kings 5). He could hardly wait to try it on, I'm sure . . . sin's big plans. Haman could achieve his power-driven success with Mordecai out of the way . . . sin's big plans.

Sin deserts the project mid-heartbreak. Women are pulled away from their families to find themselves in no-man's land. Sin-induced disease robs the young of lifelong relationships. Babies are conceived to fathers who have dropped off the planet. The project was promising just as the cheap plastic toy, but as with the toy, it is soon deserted.

Bring Christ Your Broken Life

Mama's "well worth it" phrase is passed on to my kids at yard sales and arcades. But I hope it will be passed on in the bigger picture. If Satan promises you something for nothing, that something is usually worth it—nothing! And the nickel you pay will turn out to be an irretrievable fortune.

But there is one overwhelming consolation. Most businessmen will not buy back that which is worthless and broken. Christ will.

> *O wretched man that I am! Who will deliver me from this body of death? I thank God—through Jesus Christ our Lord!*
>
> —Romans 7:24–25

Something for YOU to Do . . .

1. Contrast being rich with desiring to be rich. What is the difference? Can the two coexist?

2. What are some yellow cones which warn of impending fall that you recognize in people's lives from experience?

3. Review the biblical examples of lives ruined for a few minutes of fun that we discussed in this chapter. Name other biblical characters who fall into this category. How did their few minutes of fun pan out in consequences?

4. What constitutes a senseless desire?

5. Does it lend credibility to a statement when someone says, "I swear" or "I swear to God"? Why would James see this as a danger of falling into condemnation?

6. What kind of dancing do you think Herod's stepdaughter was doing to provoke such a promise? Could it be akin to any of the dances we see two thousand years later? What long-term results do we expect from small children's dance classes?

～ Spark Plugs ～

And speaking of plastic wrap · · ·

It seems to me we have come a long way in advancing a lot of things for world leaders and housewives. The problem of getting tangled up in the curly cord on the phone and having to lay it down while you try to reach the waffle iron in time has pretty much forever been solved. No more shuffling paper grocery bags while you struggle to put the key in the hole to unlock the car door. No grieving sessions over the camera back coming undone in the middle of the unity candle ceremony, thus exposing the entire roll.

Life is good now, except for the plastic wrap. I live in the city of engineers, rocket scientists who peer over your shoulder when you change batteries. They mill around the kitchen at the church fellowships with seven pens and a tire gauge in their pockets looking for an easily-solvable design flaw in a small appliance.

"Haven't you guys been able to do anything about this yet?" I wave the abused plastic wrap box in their faces. There are wads of plastic wrap surrounding my undone service project. I envision myself lying on a settee explaining it all to a man with a Ph.D. and a Ferrari:

"It all began with a box. It was one of those with a saw blade attached under the 'Open here' flap. I was okay with that at first, because I knew ultimately the blade had a better purpose than just to cut my finger. I was deceived by that, but let's back up. There was a roll of plastic wrap there inside the box. It had no beginning and no end. It was just a mass of continuous wrinkled transparent film. I wondered how one might begin to unravel this mystery. I soon found out. The makers do ensure that there's one small, loose corner place. I dug my fingernail under this which began the mass futility. It's here that, as most people can attest, the plastic wrap starts to unroll, not uniformly across the roll, but tearing in a spiral producing a cone shape that could truly only wrap a very long set of toenail clippers. It was then I hoped to use the blade on the box to cut away this initial disaster and start all over. Though it can cut flesh, it generally is not meant to actually cut the plastic wrap, but rather to use the force behind the yank intended at severing the wrap from itself to actually catapult the roll to the floor where it unrolls both gladly and liberally.

"The engineers began to argue among themselves about the degree of the angle of my wrist at the initial point of yank while one retrieved a pen from his pocket which at closer examination, doubled as a pair of scissors and dog leash. I used the scissors part to cut what should have been squares from the roll. I was sure if I wedged one end of the wrap between my abdomen and the counter and carefully held the roll under my chin while I cut a piece holding it with all my might, this time it would not, you know . . . But it did.

"That's when I first developed this twitch as I recall. It was slight at first, but then I began to unwad the little balls of plastic wrap on the counter and try to wrap them on the paper plates. Someone tell me how it is that the plastic wrap will stick to everything in its path, mostly itself, and then refuse to stick to the plate it was intended for. Do you think there could be a little terrorist inside that roll somewhere?"

I gave up plastic wrap early in my marriage, completely content with stale and dirty snacks. Who cares about food preservation? Preserving my mind was more important. Then phase two occurred. If they couldn't get me on the practical, I would surely give in to the whimsical. So they began to make it in colors, and I decided to give it another shot, but what I ended up with was leftover confusion: Is this molded cornbread or just festive? Is this the pink Jell-O you were asking for, or is this a muffin under pink wrap?

> Wads of plastic wrap surround my undone service project.

As Solomon said, this too was vanity. Then came phase three. The food shower caps came out. Though quite a bit more expensive (I now could only afford to cover food once a week), these solved some of the earlier issues of over-self-adhesiveness and personal injuries. But a new problem replaced it. I found myself in the shower, my head covered with what should have been on the poppy seed chicken. This would have been humorous were it not for the concern over what must be sitting in the church basement over the casserole for the grieving family.

Oh, I know, I know, there are the little bags now. I say little bags because most people, and these are oddly enough adults, call them baggies or zippies or in the case of totally verbal people, zippy baggies. These are an improvement over the old stuff, but it's just hard to fit a whole turkey skeleton in one.

But then again, given the alternative, I think it'll fit.

Top: Johnnia washing dishes in her first house after marriage, Pelham Heights in Calhoun County, Alabama.

Bottom: Johnnia peeking over a ledge at Cheaha Mountain.

CHAPTER 3

You Can't Have Your Cake and Eat It, Too

Instant Gratification

*Now faith is the substance of things hoped
for, the evidence of things not seen.*

—Hebrews 11:1

I was homesick. It was my first time to go to summer camp. I missed my mama, and I just wanted to go home right then . . . except I didn't want to miss the skating night. Camp was a place where you had to walk up-hill to the bathhouse in the dark, where everyone but you vowed they had seen vampire bats and ana-condas. At home, the bathroom was inside and there were only giant mosquitoes. My mama was at home, and she would know whether anacondas were really, truly under my cabin. I was decided . . . I would leave for home in the morning . . . but I didn't want to miss the watermelon hike. At camp, you had to sing all eighteen stanzas of "There's a hole in the bottom of the sea" backwards in order to get your mail. There would be a note from my grandmother "Dunca", but I couldn't read it without Mama to decipher the handwriting. I really needed to go home . . . but I would miss talent night. Drew was going to pull a string through his head from one ear to the other at talent night.

My counselor had watched me pack and unpack the teddy bear one too many times. "Celine," she finally said, "You can't have your cake and eat it, too."

Hey, I thought, *that's just what my mama would have said!*

• •

It's a weird phrase if you put too much thought into it. Of course you can have your cake and eat it. Have some cake, eat some cake—same thing to me. I was practically in college before I got it. Of course the deal is that you can't eat your cake, and then go back to the cake and still enjoy its beauty on the plate.

It's not much of a dilemma, is it? Hmmm. Eat cake. Look at cake. Eat cake. Look at cake. There's only one viable answer—eat the cake!

Cake and life share some things in common. They both can be messy, fattening, and expensive. But when it comes to the dilemma of indulging now at the risk of destroying what can be kept forever, life and cake are completely different. If it's only cake, I say eat it and not a minute too soon. But if it's life, consider long and hard, pray without ceasing, choose on your tiptoes and with gloves on—very carefully. It's what my mama and yours were saying often when they cautioned, "You can't have your cake and eat it, too."

Instant Gratification: *The Price of Eating Now*

The generations of my lifespan are all about eating cake *now*. We term it *instant gratification*. We must have instant oatmeal, instant coffee, instant messaging . . . we can put a little pill-looking thing in the sink, and poof!—we have an instant foam dinosaur. The number one complaint I hear about fast food restaurants is not that the food tastes like Styrofoam or that your shoes stick to the floor, but simply that the fast food is not fast enough. We order our Internet service based on speed, and we will pay a substantial difference in price for a fraction of a second. We echo Veruca Salt in Willie Wonka's factory, "I want it now!"[1]

But is this really a generational problem or just a new verse of an old song? Esau would go back a few years, wouldn't he? Like to the book of Genesis, literally translated "beginning." Esau ordered some fast food, just a bowl of stew, and he simply could not wait. His shrewd brother made a deal with him. He could have the stew, but he would have to trade his birthright for it. His entire inheritance? For a bowl of soup? Was he out of his mind? No more than your average American. He just wanted instant gratification. He ate the cake at the price of not having it.

- *Instant gratification forfeits delayed reward.* It's easy to talk about how foolish Esau was when we're holding the flipchart in front of the Bible class. Monday through Saturday, his fault is not so obvious as we constantly are presented with the same offer—some gratification now or much greater gratification deferred. We have an unfathomable inheritance. The street of gold and the many-roomed mansion that await us in heaven are inviting. But greater far is the sure knowledge that inside that mansion are no tears, no sadness, no emptiness, no loneliness. It's quite a contrast to some of the high end mansions here—physically elaborate dream homes filled with broken dreams.

  Before the cake incident, Esau was first in line to receive a huge inheritance. "Abram was very rich in livestock, in sliver and in gold" (Genesis 13:2), and Esau was the firstborn son of the only son—at least the only heir (Genesis 25:5). This one moment of "wanting it now" changed all of that, and the rest of the Bible unfolds based on Jacob's assuming the firstborn position.

- *Instant gratification has no lasting benefits.* The "eat cake" philosophy works that way. Esau's inheritance was nothing but a cardboard box compared to the inheritance that awaits Christians (1 Peter 1:4, Revelation 21:7). I can't think of benefits that would be any less permanent than a bowl of stew (except cake). It was both mouth-watering and finger-licking I'm sure. As Esau's stomach panged with hunger, his head may have been hurting, and he might have become a little shaky and irritable. His body was signaling mealtime. All these symptoms were immediately soothed as the stew went down. He was instantly gratified.

---

1 Mel Stuart, Director, *Willie Wonka and the Chocolate Factory*, 1971.

Then came the aftertaste that would last the rest of his life. He was no longer the heir. The deal was sealed. The stew was swallowed. There was no going back. And yet within a few hours, if Esau's system was normal, he was hungry again. He had traded his inheritance for something that had no lasting benefits.

Instant gratification puts the common above the valuable. How common is stew? On the Fourth of July in north Alabama, you can buy a gallon at every volunteer fire station and corner senior center. When times are bad and you can't afford a loaf of bread or a roof overhead, you can always stand in the soup line. When the pantry is bare and the kids are hungry, what do we do? We pull the week's leftovers out of the fridge and make a stew. It's that common. Something tells me it wasn't too rare in Esau's time either. I venture this partially because even in a famine in 2 Kings 4, Elisha instructs to make a stew, and the men are able to gather enough (without a miracle in this case) to carry out the command.

Esau traded his inheritance for the very common. Veruca Salt's "I want it now" attitude is just one of many instant gratification moments in the book and subsequent movies. In *Charlie and the Chocolate Factory* (2005), even Charlie struggles at one point, at which time his poverty-stricken grandfather says, "There's plenty of money out there. They print more every day, but this ticket, there's only five of them in the whole world, and that's all there's ever going to be. Only a dummy would give this up for something as common as money. Are you a dummy?"[1]

Am I a dummy? Would I give up a rare ticket for common money? Those who have had their sins washed away have become heirs to the kingdom (Romans 8:17). We have a golden ticket. Who would want to trade it for something so common as dollars? Be careful.

Instant gratification robs us of clearly thought-out decisions. What if Esau had waited? Esau was obviously able to prepare a far better meal. Why did Isaac love Esau more? Genesis 25:28 says it was because he ate of his game. One of Isaac's final requests was to have Esau prepare a meal "such as I love" (Genesis 27:4). He had experience at the grill. He could have enjoyed a far more delicious meal with no lifelong consequences, but he would have to wait.

---

1 Director Tim Burton, *Charlie and the Chocolate Factory*, 2005.

Esau's judgment was impaired. The passage tells us that on top of being hungry, he was weary. Have you ever tried to make an important decision when you were dead tired? It's not a happy situation. Confusion and frustration prevail, and emotional outbursts in one form or another emerge. Isn't it amazing that in the morning, with lots of prayer and clear thinking, the prospects are much brighter? It's quite possible that Esau was emotional over the stew.

Emotional decisions are not good ones, and they can end in our trading the valuable for the common. What would make me happy at the time? That's an emotional decision. Instant gratification decisions do not consider the long-run, and we are robbed of the ability for good sense to prevail.

High-pressure decisions are also not good ones. Jacob gave Esau an immediate ultimatum. His words were, "Sell me your birthright as of this day." Satan likes to operate in the high-pressure boiler. We are convinced through his tactics that if we do not yield right here and right now, it will be a missed opportunity. Whatever it is that we want—success, popularity, love, fame, a business contract—that opportunity is right now, and we are going to have to compromise values to make it happen. No sell of birthright? No stew. As of this day. Decide now. It would be a missed opportunity, all right. He took the opportunity for the stew—on the spot. He missed the opportunity for a valuable inheritance.

Would I give up a rare ticket for common money?

Instant gratification had robbed Esau of a clearly thought-out decision. It has done the same for so many, even until today. In the heat of the moment, Achan wanted instant gratification—gold, silver, clothing (Joshua 7:21). He was so, so close to his inheritance. Forty years the children of Israel wandered in the wilderness, but that long futile era was over. Achan was among those who had crossed over and conquered Jericho. The inheritance was eminent, but he traded it for the instant and the common.

Inheritance Wins over Instant Gratification

Life is a vapor (James 4:14). Our inheritance is eminent. We are out of our minds to trade it for anything this side of the Jordan. We have to stop making decisions based on any benefits we will receive here and now.

In the 1970s, there was a Girl Scout camp planned for the night of our gospel meeting. I was a child, but I had recently been baptized into Christ. It was decision time, and it was the earliest one I remember in my Christian journey. I opted to save the cake. At least that time, the inheritance won out over the instant gratification, and I have never forgotten it. As I talk to other Baby Boomers, I hear the same story with different details . . . a concert on a Wednesday, a tournament during evening worship, a Sunday Baccalaureate, prom . . . the list goes on. Some opted to eat the cake, others to save it, but the amazing part to me is that every one of them remembers it in vivid color. I either hear, "I went, and I had a miserable time" or "I didn't go, and I never regretted it."

As young people, the conviction was deep. Our hearts were cut. We understood that we couldn't have our cake and eat it, too. What happened? It seems that those of us who are closer to the inheritance would battle the instant gratification with a stronger passion. We're almost there. We're too big to give in to cake.

For what is your life? It is even a vapor that appears
for a little time and then vanishes away.

—James 4:14

Wait for the Reward

What's your favorite cake? Mine is cheesecake, and it's hard to turn down, but I can do it. I can do it when my schedule is not off, and I have nourished myself with healthy meals and snacks. I can think about the dress I'm trying to fit into or a future weigh-in. But if I'm weak, hungry, and stressed, I will eat the cake every time. As Christians, it's important to nourish ourselves with spiritual food—God's word. It's important to strengthen ourselves. This comes through praying, studying the Bible, surrounding ourselves with Christians, and immersing ourselves in Christian work. But there's more – the truth is that nothing strengthens us like adversity. It's hard to thank God for adversity, but we are told more than once to rejoice because of it. It keeps us from eating the cake. It keeps us focused on the inheritance.

I'm told of a time in recent American history—perhaps your parents lived through it—when families waited for harvest. When the crop came in, the children would get new shoes for winter, but they must wait for the harvest. As a result, I have heard more than one older person recall with emotion the occasion of a new pair of shoes. It was a big deal. In our culture, kids have to get to the mall to get into the latest athletic shoe trend immediately. They're so excited as they rip into the new box. They do a few athletic feats down the escalator as they tell strangers about their Z-23s or whatever they're called this time. Within a month, the shoes are lost, or at best forgotten. Within three months, they've got to have the latest style all over again.

Wasn't there greater reward in waiting for the harvest? More than once, Jesus refers to the harvest as the end of the world. According to Matthew 13, at that time the righteous will shine forth as the sun. Isn't that worth waiting for, especially when contrasted with those who gave in to sin? "The Son of Man will send out His angels, and they will gather out of His kingdom all things that offend, and those who practice lawlessness, and will cast them into the furnace of fire. There will be wailing and gnashing of teeth." (vv. 41–42).

Heaven is a place that we can't see. Though we have been given the best word pictures imaginable, and we have full assurance that God's children have a reserved spot; it is in the best sense a surprise.

Wait with Perseverance

With our technology, we're not accustomed to "wait and see." We cannot wait nine months to know the baby's gender. Tell us now, with pictures please. What would my den look like with this color paint and this trim? I can see a picture immediately. We no longer have to imagine what the person on the other end of the call is wearing. We are a culture of cake-eaters and not cake-savers. When it comes to life dilemmas and spiritual decisions, we have to hold tight to our inheritance which we cannot yet physically see. "But if we hope for what we do not see, we eagerly wait for it with perseverance" (Romans 8:25). Eagerly wait, and persevere.

As a photographer, my lot falls to deal with many brides and grooms. Of those I have photographed, the majority are already in a live-together arrangement before the wedding. As I photograph the intricate, beautiful cake, I sometimes imagine it as a half-devoured, jagged, crumbly mess. The cake has already been eaten, and it's like Mama and my camp counselor said, "You can't have your cake and eat it, too."

Though I'm all for marriage among scripturally eligible couples who are truly committed to one another, and I believe God fully forgives premarital sin in His repentant children, we need to warn our young of the dangers of a prematurely eaten cake. There are many sources of information concerning the obvious physical consequences, but couples need to understand that there are also relational consequences. Sex offers a married couple a special bond of intimacy. If a couple has been sexually active with one another before marriage, the marriage offers them no more closeness and intimacy than they had when they were single. This lack of bonding leads to mistrust, and often a spouse begins to resent that they were not respected enough, and were taken advantage of sexually before marriage. If there were other sexual partners in the premarital past, there is also a heightened insecurity hampered by comparisons or perceived comparisons.

While sexual sin is a graphic example of choosing to eat cake, rather than save it, it is only one of a host of temptations aimed at making us forfeit the prize. We can sell our soul for a promotion at work; for acceptance into a crowd that doesn't share God's views; for a one-time social event when we hate to be conspicuous. Really? Can it happen that nonchalantly? It happened for a bowl of soup.

Don't.

See to it that no one fails to obtain the grace of God . . .
like Esau, who sold his birthright for a single meal.
—Hebrews 12:15–16 ESV

Something for YOU to Do . . .

1. Think of something in your life that you really waited for. Was it worth the wait? What makes it so memorable?

2. List some specific things, other than the ones in this chapter, which people have traded for their inheritance.

3. What is the value in adversity? What scriptures back this idea?

4. What factors under Esau's control would have helped him to make a better decision?

5. How do you think intimacy and closeness are hampered if a couple is sexually active before marriage?

6. Discuss other relational problems in a marriage when sex has preceded it. How can a married couple best deal with these issues?

7. What are some further parallels between stew and the sins which so easily distract us?

8. How should we deal with big decisions when we are tired? What are some alternatives to making decisions in a tired state?

9. In your lifetime, how have you observed the evolution of instant gratification? List some "wait" activities of the past that have become today's "instants."

10. Some things are common like stew and dollars. What about a "once in a lifetime" opportunity? Are there some opportunities which should be examined more carefully because they have so much to offer in this life? Are these a greater temptation? Should they be?

Spark Plugs

And speaking of camp ...

Now remind me again why we do this. We call it summer Bible camp, but that's because the phrase "straight jacket" was already taken. At age eleven, it's a whole different place than at age, say, 44 or so.

At eleven, camp was the symbol of freedom. Jerry would start the week by saying "At Maywood, we have only one rule." He may as well have said, "There is an anaconda under the bleachers" because to us, his speech was over right then and there: *only one rule?* Though the one rule was "do right," from then on, the name "Maywood" could have been more correctly pronounced "Mayhem." This rule did not say anything about frogs in counselors' suitcases or sliding off the roof of the mess hall.

Reflecting on this at age, say, 44 or so, I think we should give some serious attention to amendments to the "do right" rule. At age 44 or so, I'm wondering if we should have a piece of legislation about keeping Cokes cold in the commode tank and hiding counselors' underwear in the meat freezer.

I've approached camp from every angle. My adult career at camp began as a counselor. The name implies being a listening ear and a shoulder to cry on for homesick campers. That was the good part, but what I found out was that I didn't have enough shoulders or ears to go around, and that pancakes with dishrags inside are okay if you use enough syrup.

It turns out that the crafts directors were retiring that year. Could this opening be the answer to my prayers? I could imagine that no one in the crafts quarters was on Ritalin, and the craft hut was at the bottom of the hill instead of the very peak. I got the job based on the fact that I could make a snake out of Play-Doh.

It didn't take long to figure out the impetus for early retirement of craft directors. We made critter cages that first year. Who knew that the boys' hill could capture the entire north Alabama population of the wasp species? Who would have thought when I said "paint whatever you like," they would have understood this to mean the camp dog? But this was the good news. The bad news was that some gifted engineer, who I wish had never set foot on a campground, designed the laundry room adjacent to the crafts station with—get this!—the dryer vents blowing hot air directly into the craft shelter . . . in July.

This would have worked well under normal circumstances, because who washes clothes at camp anyway? The plan is to wear the same shirt until it is completely too filthy to look at, and then turn it inside out and wear it the rest of the week. The dryer would have been no problem except for the outbreak of head lice in all of the cabins. These were desperate head lice, even attacking Billy, the counselor who had hair only if you count the fuzzy veins. All of the campers' clothing had to be treated, washed, and dried on the high-heat setting. I was a homesick camper.

> Desperate head lice attacked Billy who had hair only if you count the fuzzy veins.

Then I learned that the sports director was retiring. The next Sunday the camp director approached my husband after his sermon. "What's the white round thing called that you hit with a stick?"

"A baseball?" my husband asked.

"Good! You're qualified!"

I joined my husband on this trek. Though we didn't know third base from tofu, we were ping-pong ball sergeants. I would have kept the coaching position had we not found out the head counselor was retiring.

How hard could it be? Just making sure everyone has a bed, gets to stay in the cabin with her cousin, and has a counselor. Here's where the straight jacket part comes in.

After a few years of this, we moved to Mississippi and tried to live a normal post-camp life, but there was something missing—stunt night.

We call it that only because no Christian alive could call it a talent show with a clear conscience.

We reentered the camp zone in Sardis, Mississippi, thrilled to be back among chocolate milk ear washes and toothpaste toupees on bald directors. How is it that this night is as far removed from talent as Sri Lanka from Coney Island, and yet we would just about trade in Springsteen tickets to be there? It has to do with the fact that it is entirely dedicated to embarrassing the camp staff. We wouldn't miss it for the world should the camp cooks be exploited, and we couldn't afford to miss it if, heaven forbid, our own likeness appeared in pillow-stuffed sweatpants and pipe-cleaner glasses.

Through the years, we've found that all Christian camps share basic tenets like taco salad and long hikes, and that those hikes get more difficult each year until this year the hike leader whose first initial is David, announced, "We want all the campers to understand that it is not required to go on the hike, and in fact, we are publicly discouraging campers from going on the hike." It didn't work—the hikers showed up in droves. But those in the 44-or-so group brought nurses' excuses from home. Forgive me, I'm suspicious, but why, as I sat in my lawn chair with my nurse's excuse, did I watch the hikers depart, not on foot but in two overcrowded vans? Has the word *hiking* changed meaning in recent years?

And speaking of this 44-or-so crowd, does anyone wonder why preachers are so drawn to the Christian camp culture? Why would they leave behind an air-conditioned church building, hospital parking passes, and *Bulletin Digest*? This: It is the only time of year they get to preach in SpongeBob pajama pants. Not only that, but they find a responsive audience. At home, unfortunately, we are preoccupied with physical distractions—fashion consciousness, temperature settings, and looming light fixtures. At camp these distractions are gone, and the preacher has us where he wants us. We laugh and cry at all the right places. What he doesn't understand is that we're basket-cases by midweek. We laugh when a raindrop hits a gutter, and we cry when the corndog falls off the stick.

But this captive audience brings the preachers back, and back. Every Christian camp I know of has an old preacher that we're just sure is going to pass any minute. We get a little nervous when the vultures start circling on the way to the baptism hole.

But on the other hand, we wouldn't want camp life without them. What will we do if Richard ever retires? His innate inventiveness takes care of all the missing amenities at camp. This is why, in answer to the question of so many, there is—I promise—a washing machine on the roof of the mess hall strapped to a pole with a bell on it. This way, you can push a button from the kitchen which activates the agitator which vibrates the pole, and voila—the dinner bell!

Only at camp.

So back to my initial quandary—remind me again why we do this. What is the purpose of camp? Besides eleven-year olds losing everything they packed, were born with, and made during the week?

There's something about getting away from the world that week. There's something about hanging out in pajama pants and dirty tee shirts that dramatically lessens the pull of fashion magazines and internet pop-ups. Could it be that it's the only time all year that the familiar words of the song really reflect our being: "Jesus in the morning, Jesus in the evening, Jesus when the sun goes down"?

What's a little rag in a pancake, a few hundred wasps, and an outbreak of head lice compared with the moment in time when a young heart surrenders to Christ? Sign me up. I'll be there on the top bunk . . . 'til the vultures start circling on the way to the baptism hole.

Young Johnnia holding niece, Alice Smith, in the mill village, Jacksonville, Alabama.

Top: Johnnia, 1951.

Bottom: Johnnia, age 8, with her brother Bobby Duncan, age 3, 1937.

CHAPTER 4

IF ALL YOUR FRIENDS JUMPED OFF A BUILDING . . .

Chameleons

You shall not follow a crowd to do evil.

—Exodus 23:2

Remember the era? We put gel in our hair just to make it stick up. A white tee shirt, a man's blazer with the sleeves rolled up, some Bruce Willis sunglasses, and I was ready to go . . . except for one thing, the main thing. I had to get the bandana tied around my stonewashed jeans, just above the knee. Now I was ready. But Mama wasn't. I knew the last part of the routine by heart, "You are not going out of the house like that."

"But Mom, this is the style. All my friends are wearing this."

Okay, here it comes: *If all your friends jump off a building, are you going to do it, too?*

• •

Who thought of that? Are all moms just intrinsically born with those words engraved on the tip of their tongue? In all the years this phrase has been used, I have never seen nor heard of a group of teenagers lining up on top of a building for the jump. And yet the phrase maintains its popularity among moms everywhere.

Just once I would have like to have said, "But Mama, all your friends are saying that phrase." What would she say then, huh?

The deal is, the question answers itself. Of course, if such a thing should happen that all our friends should line up to jump off a building; of *course* we would not participate. But such a thing could never happen. Or could it?

Like the Other Nations

There is a deep chasm which really exists called hell. Many are plunging into its depths every day, and the majority of people are blindly joining in for no good reason other than "everyone else is doing it."

The elders of Israel once came to Samuel and said, "Now make us a king to judge us like all the nations" (1 Samuel 8:5). That was their whole line of reasoning: All our friends are doing it.

The answer Samuel gave them, it seems, would change their minds. He told them he was willing, but this king would eventually take their children as slaves and take their land and other possessions. Furthermore, after the takeover, Samuel warned Israel that they would cry out to the Lord in their poverty and despair, but the Lord would not hear them.

After such a direct answer, you would expect them to say, "Never mind. I think we're good," but that drive to be like everyone else superseded all reason. "No, but we will have a king over us; that we also may be like all the nations" (vv. 19–20).

There lies the problem: God's people wanting to be like all the other people who are not God's people. It didn't work then, and it won't work now.

*And the king was sorry, but because of his oaths
and his guests he commanded it to be given.*

—Matthew 14:9 ESV

Alternative—or Sin?

Thirty years back, people believed that homosexual partnerships were a perversion of the natural sexual relationship. All our friends believed that, so we, God's people, believed it, too. Now people around us have become "enlightened," the homosexual movement has strengthened, and it is no longer socially permissible to view homosexuality as a sin.

As the views of the people around us have changed, many of those claiming Christianity have altered their stance as well. The Bible is as clear on this teaching as Mama was about what I could not wear out of the house (Romans 1:26–27; 1 Corinthians 6:9; 1 Kings 14:24; Deuteronomy 23:17; Leviticus 18:22; 20:13). The problem is that all our friends are accepting this as the right thing now. It's just one choice among many alternatives, not a wrong act.

Considering that this acceptance is directly converse to God's teaching, yes Mama, it does seem that if all our friends jumped off the top of a building, we'd line up, too.

"I Haven't Seen It"

In 1939 the world was shocked by the presence of a four-letter word in a big screen picture, a word that the MPAA rating system now refers to as very mild profanity. It was a shock then; it's mild profanity now—so mild that Christians don't blink. The word is welcome in our living rooms, as long as it's coming from the TV. Since most shows contain this, it's reasoned that everyone is doing it, and we just can't avoid it. We've even taken it up a few notches since 1939 and now allow other stronger expletives that were once taboo. I'm more than a little concerned at the prevalent attitude that something may not be suitable for the kids, so we need to be careful to watch it only when they're not around. Something else my mama often said was, "If it's not fit for the kids, it's not fit for the adults."

In 1 Timothy 4:12 Paul expects Timothy to be an example in speech and in purity. Philippians 4:8 gives us a list of things to mentally absorb and think on. Interestingly, "whatsoever things are pure" makes the list, and profanity does not. It's okay to be in a crowd of people who are discussing the number one grossing movie, and to say, "I haven't seen it." It's not a requirement to partake in the entertainment that "all our friends are doing." It's not a requirement to jump off the building.

*I have sinned, for I have transgressed the
commandment of the Lord and your words,
because I feared the people and obeyed their voice.*

—I Samuel 15:24

Popsicle Gym Suit

Furthermore, it's not a requirement to dress the way all our friends are dressing. Mama made that pretty clear with the bandana thing. I'm beginning to wonder if Christians realize that it's possible to get wet fully dressed. We do that at baptisms, don't we? It would pretty much stun us if the preacher stepped into the baptistry with swim trunks and no shirt on next Sunday, wouldn't it? It would hardly be appropriate. What makes it appropriate then at the pool, the beach, or the water slide? Simply this: that everyone else is dressed that way.

It's not a requirement to jump off the building.

If all the shorts at the mall come halfway up the thigh or better, did you know you can buy long pants instead? As a matter of policy, our summer Bible camp has a requirement that all campers wear long pants. Amazingly, we have not lost one single camper to heat stroke. Have we forgotten that cut-offs, as the name implies, are pants that are cut off? This means you can cut them off literally anywhere on the whole leg of the pants, not just right beneath the crotch.

You see, it's not really that there are no alternatives to skimpy clothing which shows a lot of skin. It's that we want to wear what everyone else is wearing, and the fact that everyone else is wearing it somehow makes it okay.

Your gym teacher may tell you that your past-puberty child has to dress out in very short shorts for P.E. As a Christian, your child can politely ask her teacher to let her wear similar shorts which are longer, sweatpants or wind pants. The teacher will most likely cooperate. I remember my poor sister had to actually make a gym suit which made her look very much like a bright blue Popsicle. Was she different? She sure was. Did she stand out? She sure did. Is that a good thing? It sure is. My sister learned from the gym suit experience that she didn't have to be a building jumper.

Stand Out from the Crowd

As grueling as they are, these ultimatums the devil hands us, intending that we teach our children early on to compromise values, can actually be huge blessings if we use them the right way. We turn the tables on the devil instead, teaching our children instead that it's okay to stand out from the crowd. Different is good.

Is sin cultural? Can something that used to be sinful no longer be? Some things are appropriate in one culture, but not in another. It is inappropriate in India to eat with your left hand. That is not acceptable behavior culturally in India, but it is not sinful. Upon visiting the Philippines, the American men in our group were asked not to wear athletic shoes with a formal shirt in worship. The combination showed disrespect, but even there, it did not qualify as sinful. When our founders signed the Declaration of Independence, many of them wore white wigs with pony tails. Congressmen just don't show up in those now. It's not appropriate; it was cultural.

Sins of Culture or Sins of the Flesh?

God wants us to consider the culture in our decisions. That's why he instructed the first century Christians to eat meat or not eat meat based on whether or not it would offend those tied to the culture they were in (1 Corinthians 8).

However, Galatians 5:19–21 talks about the sins of the flesh, not the offenses of the culture. The opening phrase says, "Now the works of the flesh are manifest." They are obvious, they are evident, they are clear. The list includes indecency (lasciviousness), wild parties with dancing (revellings), and drunkenness. These are everywhere in our culture, and the "good guys" in our movies are partaking. Spiderman, Superman, and Batman usually indulge in a few of these manifest works of the flesh. But then again, they usually jump off buildings too, don't they?

This list of cross-cultural flesh-works also includes things like strife, jealousies, and factions. In all cultures worldwide and in every generation, it seems that everyone is bickering, whether in the kitchen, across the fast-food counter, or in the Senate. Christians, though, don't have to do what everyone else is doing.

When I bow down in the temple of Rimmon, may the Lord please pardon your servant in this thing.
—2 Kings 5:18

A Chosen Generation

Finally, I think there is one glaring contemporary parallel to the attitude of Israel in 1 Samuel 8. They were God's special people; yet they just wanted to be like all the other nations. They had grown tired of the conspicuous calling and of following God's command. Why couldn't they just follow men like everyone else?

Those in the Lord's church should be more than satisfied with having one body, one Spirit, one hope, one Lord, one faith, one baptism (Ephesians 4:4–5), but many are not. We see the "nations" around us, many religious bodies with differing baptisms and differing faiths. Some have grown tired of the conspicuous calling and following God's command. If other churches have manmade practices and traditions contrary to God's teaching, why can't we? We want a king with a little "k," too.

We want to speak of senior pastors, too, just like everyone else does. We want to have worship leaders. It's awkward to say we're not part of a denomination—just the Lord's church. How normal is that? It's a little embarrassing to say "our" church was founded two thousand years ago. Can't we refer to it as a movement, a heritage, or a tradition? That sounds much more manmade.

When our goal becomes to be like everyone else, we lose sight of the value of the pure doctrine of the Word that, at its premise, calls us to be different: "But you are a chosen generation, a royal priesthood, a holy nation, His own special people, that you may proclaim the praises of Him who called you out of darkness into His marvelous light" (1 Peter 2:9).

The Narrow Gate

The fact that all of our friends are doing it should be a red flag for scrutiny. It's like the tip-off we get when we're driving down a road in unfamiliar territory. Something gets our attention, and we say out loud, "Uh-oh, I think I'm on the wrong road." Well about that, Jesus says, "Enter by the narrow gate; for wide is the gate and broad is the way that leads to destruction."

If we're using for our standard what everyone else around us is doing, this should be a big tip-off. Jesus says only a few are on the road which leads to life, and many are on the road to destruction. If something seems right because everyone else is doing it, then uh-oh, I think we're on the wrong road.

And that road appears to be leading to the roof of a giant skyscraper.

Enter by the narrow gate; for wide is the gate and broad is the way that leads to destruction, and there are many who go in by it. Because narrow is the gate and difficult is the way which leads to life, and there are few who find it.

—Matthew 7:13–14

Something for YOU to Do . . .

1. Take a look at Galatians 5:19–21. Which of these sins are the most prevalent even among the "good guys"? What can we do to ensure we don't become building jumpers in these areas?

2. What should be our attitude toward homosexuality? Is it any bigger or worse than the sins listed with it in 1 Corinthians 6:9? How can we extend the grace of God to those involved while standing firm against the practice?

3. What about Mama's saying, "If it's not fit for the kids, it's not fit for the grown-ups"? Do you agree or disagree? How does this fit in with Philippians 4:8?

4. What have some in the church compromised so that they might be "like all the nations"?

5. Look at Romans 12:1. What are you sacrificing that sets you apart from the building jumpers? What adjectives are in this verse? Do they describe a sacrifice in your life?

And speaking of movies . . .

Who can afford them? I mean, of course, besides Bill Gates and my dentist? That's why we love summer Tuesdays, when the theater has free-movie mornings, showing a movie that everybody on the planet, except for us, has seen three times. So the object of the game at this event is to see who can say, "Watch this part; this is good!" exactly one more time than Brett Favre has retired.

This is when I would like to stand and explain to the entire audience at once that the purpose of coming to a movie is, believe it or not, to watch it. It is completely unnecessary to repeatedly instruct the viewers to watch since they are enclosed in a dark theater facing an unavoidably large and loud screen, and it would be impractical to try to do anything else at this point other than watch.

And what is it about popcorn? How is it that I can have boxes of microwavable popcorn that have been in my pantry since the Clinton administration, totally ignored, but we can walk through the theater door and in less than twenty seconds, the entire family has a fierce craving for popcorn? "But Mama, I am sooo hungry," the children pull at my conscience, as if a bucket of popcorn (mostly air) is going to provide sustaining nutrients to their diet.

I glance at the concession stand marquis, and this is precisely when I remember why it is that a sane, for-profit business entrepreneur will offer to show a movie to the general susceptible public for free. "Are these prices in American currency?" I ask.

"We have a special today," the OPS (official popcorn scooper) answers, "You can get a combo for just an arm and upper thigh rather than the whole leg." With a special like that, I can see why the line weaves around most of the Louisiana Purchase and people are good with missing half the movie as long as they get that popcorn fix.

"Would you like a drink with that? You can get a free refill on the dumpster-size."

The contents of the dumpster cup quickly move directly into the bladder so that the morning of a free relaxing movie has suddenly changed to the all-out world's largest bathroom relay marathon. When my kids were little, we decided to take in a showing of *The Wizard of Oz* while on vacation outside Memphis. There were four tiny impatient bladders between them, all too young to go to the bathroom unaccompanied. The opening credits were quite good, and then this is what I got from the rest of the movie.

"Oh, Auntie Em."
"Which way to the bathroom?"
"Follow the yellow brick road."
"We're not in Kansas anymore."
"No, we're in the bathroom."
"Do you want to go with us?"
"To the bathroom?"
"She's gotta go again."
"Which old witch?"
"It's the monkeys."
"TOTO!"
"There's no place like the bathroom."

The next vacation we found a dollar movie in Chattanooga—only it was a documentary. I talked the whole family into it, saying it would be a great educational experience. They have never let me forget that we sat through the entire gestational period of a penguin—63 days.

> Are these prices in American currency?

But back to the free Tuesday thing. These movies have proven to actually be pretty good, but we've learned to get there way early or we'll have to watch the alternative. "Hi, we're here to see *Polar Express*."

"I'm sorry, there are no seats, but we have *Hamstermania* on screen 8. It's a terrific movie about an orphaned child who wins the state championship with the help of his hamster, and it has some great bathroom humor."

"Do you realize how many times we have been to a state championship with a gifted animal in this very theatre? And I got all the bathroom humor I ever care to see in *The Wizard of Oz*."

So now, we set the alarm before daylight to try to beat the daycare buses who I think actually camp out the night before because, after all, what care provider would not sit through—key word being "sit"—two penguin gestational periods if it meant missing show and tell—key word being "tell."

Because we are a large family, there are never enough seats together, but we scatter throughout doing sign language across the theatre, spelling out, "Watch this!" and "Do you want a sip from the dumpster?"

Momentarily, I consider paying full price for a movie, imagining us sitting together with cup holders that will hold the cup, our bladders patiently holding the contents.

"Look, Mom! Next week they're showing *Revenge of the Daycare Buses*."

The moment is gone.

Sparks Kids:
Miriam, Abram,
Mattianne, and
Enoch, 2004.

CHAPTER 5

PLEASE LET ME TELL JUST ONE LIE

A Meek and Quiet Spirit

*She pestered him daily with her words and pressed
him, so that his soul was vexed to death.*

—Judges 16:16

"The other day," Mama began.

"It wasn't the other day. It was yesterday," I corrected her.

"I was talking to Estelle and Lois in the parking lot," she continued.

"No, Lois wasn't there, but Sherry was," I corrected again.

"Anyway, Estelle had just returned from Panama City—"

"It was Destin, Mama."

"Please," Mama said, "Let me tell just *one* lie."

• •

Whether or not every word of the preceding conversation actually took place, I can't remember. But I can remember this. The last six words did—over and over again. Mama's great sense of humor once again triumphed over the ordinary reprimand. In her words, "Let me tell just one lie," there was a great truth—the truth that keeping my mouth shut is more beneficial most times than being right or noticed.

I find myself frequently enumerating the things I don't have time for, but Solomon enumerates his famous list of things that there *is* a time for in Ecclesiastes 3:1–8. Among those there is a time to speak and a time to keep silent (v. 7). Most women don't have trouble with the first of these, but we forever struggle with the latter. When Mama was telling her story, this was the time to be silent.

God Takes Notice

Standing at a jewelry counter, it's easy to become enamored by the ornaments there. Most of the ones we are smitten by are too expensive to purchase. The more rare the materials, the greater the value. There is such an ornament that even God is smitten by, and even God thinks is expensive—"even the ornament of a meek and quiet spirit, which is in the sight of God of great price" (1 Peter 3:4 KJV). Isn't it amazing that as a woman, I can present something at the counter that is so rare that God notices and keeps his eye on it? Physical beauty just can't command an Audience such as this. Only one thing can: a meek and quiet spirit.

A meek and quiet spirit isn't necessarily characterized by shyness and silence. We know this because women are instructed to teach other women (Titus 2:4). Martha, in spite of her infamous kitchen frustration, powerfully opened her mouth on another occasion boldly and unwaveringly announcing her belief in Christ as the Savior (John 11:27). Lydia both begged and persuaded (Acts 16:15). The idea is that she wasn't going to shut up unless Paul and his companions agreed to stay. Her mouth was not shy or silent, but her spirit was meek and quiet.

> Keeping my mouth shut is often more beneficial than being right or noticed.

Holes in the Filters

We have women in our congregations that we miss when they're not around. Their wit is quick and their mouth muscles work out regularly. We usually leave the activities where they were present, feeling just a little bit better than we did when we arrived. Their exuberance rubs off on us. It doesn't mean they are in violation of 1 Peter 3:4. Have you ever been the last to arrive at an all-ladies event? When you open the door, you might experience a lot of things in the midst of the commotion there, but there is one thing you won't experience, and that's quiet.

A meek and quiet spirit isn't so much about the speech process, but about the thought process which should come first. There are muscles in our body which are involuntary, such as the heart and the stomach muscles. They work automatically without our thinking about it. The tongue is not an involuntary muscle. At least, it shouldn't be. Our brains are capable of many thoughts. Some of these are voluntarily sent through the nervous system to the tongue. Others begin and end in the brain.

The meek and quiet spirit serves as a filter, and some women's filters obviously have gigantic holes in them, so that whatever is thought is automatically said. We usually describe them like this, "She says what she thinks" or "She tells it like it is." What we mean is, her filter is broken. She's missing a meek and quiet spirit.

A meek and quiet spirit is not about inhibition, but about the Godly wisdom to know when to speak and when to be quiet.

A Time to Be Quiet

Thinking Criticism? Be Quiet!

Job's friends sat with him for seven days and seven nights without saying a word (Job 2:13). They had come to comfort him (v. 11). As long as they sat with him in his grief, it was a remarkable support system, but as soon as they opened their mouths, the fault-finding and criticism began. God was displeased with this to say the least (42:7). God is always displeased with this.

In John 12:3 Mary took the initiative to both serve and sacrifice, washing Jesus' feet, a lowly task, with her very best, fully a pound of "very costly" lotion, and drying them with her own hair. Those who took no such initiative themselves were quick to point out what should have been done instead. Jesus was not impressed with their analysis. "Let her alone," He said (v. 7).

I can just envision how excited Mary was as she brought her gift, hoping it would please her Friend and Lord. Can you imagine how Mary must have felt when, after bringing her very best in sacrifice, she received criticism?

Many women (and men) take the initiative to both serve and sacrifice. Standing around—which is what these apostles were doing—it's easy for us to point out how things might have been done differently. As we have moved around the Southeast, there is one common denominator I have found within all congregations—criticism of the janitorial staff, whether or not they are volunteers. Without fail, there are members disgruntled with cobwebs, lint, and scuff marks. These scrutinizers need to either grab a dust rag and a mop, or take Jesus' advice and "let her alone."

Criticizers completely miss the beauty and magnitude of what is going on around them. In John 5, Jesus thoroughly and instantly healed a man who had been unable to walk for 38 years! This was amazing; it was newsworthy; it was celebratory in the biggest way. The Pharisees missed it altogether. What they caught was this: the man was carrying his bed. It was the Sabbath, and if you twist the rules a little to fit your logic, carrying a bed (a rolled up lightweight mat) could be considered work. Out of this whole wonderful scene of miraculous healing, that was what they saw. If you look hard enough (and many people do) even in the midst of the best of the Lord's work, you can surely find something to criticize. You can find it, but it won't display a very meek and quiet spirit.

I have heard many such things;
Miserable comforters are you all!
—Job 16:2

Hold the "Advice." Be Quiet!

Unsolicited advice is just a fraction of a millimeter away from criticism. A young mother came to worship God one Sunday with a newborn in her arms, two toddlers pulling at her skirt, and her kindergartener skipping behind, but no husband. During the next hour, her earrings were pulled off and one of them lost, the baby was nursed, the collection plate was spilled, the songbook was dropped, a Hot Wheels rolled to the front pew, and a Cheerio was wedged in her bra. By the closing prayer, her stamina was gone and quiet tears rolled down her cheeks.

Under the guise of help, the lady in front of her said, "Can I give you some advice? Sit on them!" Real help doesn't work quite that way. Real help smiles and encourages, holds babies, and points to words of the song for kindergarteners. Real help picks up Cheerios and holds hands to the car in the parking lot.

Isn't there value in advice? Immeasurable. "A wise man will hear and increase learning, and a man of understanding will attain wise counsel" (Proverbs 1:5). But some things must accompany this advice. The first of these is experience. Unless you have gone through near identical circumstances, your advice may be faulty and most assuredly, won't be appreciated. That's why Paul tells the older women to advise the younger in Titus 2:4–5. They've been there.

Second, the advice usually must follow real, concrete help. If you've ever locked your keys in the car in a parking lot, everyone is an expert. Total strangers tell you to get a coat hanger, call the police and they'll bring a thingy over, always keep a spare key in your wallet, wrap some tape around the end of the hanger—all this advice can quickly become frustrating unless you have some real help.

> Real help smiles, encourages, holds babies, and picks up Cheerios.

Finally, the advice must be sought. Usually, if you have genuinely helped someone to the best of your ability . . . If you have changed the tire, if you have carried the child to the doctor, if you have bought the supper, if you have shown concern through some tangible act, you will have people beating down your door to get advice. Not all of them will listen because some are only in it for the free ride. But those who have a sincere heart are eager to soak in what may help them in their crisis.

There is only one way to give valuable advice, and that's to use God's Word. While every complicated situation may not be spelled out in scripture, guiding principles for relationships and decisions are.

Someone Else's Business? Be Quiet!

"A talebearer reveals secrets, but he who is of a faithful spirit conceals a matter" (Proverbs 11:13). "You shall not go about as a talebearer among your people," Leviticus 19:16 says. This is a "you shall not" from the Lord just as the Ten Commandments, six through ten. Its importance, though, is vastly minimized in our culture, even among Christians. Gossip is a little thing that we joke about as juicy. We call our curious daughters "little gossip queens."

The best answer to "have you heard" or "did you know" is simply "No." If someone says, "I'm not trying to gossip, but . . ." or "I'm only trying to help," then invite that person to do what real help does. Say something like this:

If that's true, then you're right. We do need to help as soon as possible. Let's go talk to her and find out if this is true and how we can help.

While others gossip, keep your mouth shut and your hands open. Offer help and follow through. It can come in the form of babysitting, pitching in some money for needed counseling, opening your home as a temporary housing arrangement, or just providing needed relief by saying, "Let's go out for a movie."

Let's look at Leviticus 19:16 again. Is it just coincidence that it is followed up with specific attitude advice for dealing with people? Verse 16 says not to go about as a talebearer, and then the very next verse says not to hate your brother, but in any wise—"no matter what" in our vernacular—rebuke him, or else his sin is going to be on your conscience. Put the two verses together, and you have the directive to go one-on-one face-to-face rather than up and down the street whispering and texting. How sound is that advice? The tagline on verse 16, by the way, says "I am the Lord." The Lord's directive remains the same in the New Testament (Matthew 18:15–17).

Time to Listen? Be Quiet!

A meek and quiet spirit listens. Mama wasn't the only one who had favorite phrases used over and over again. Jesus had a few favorites, too, and this was one of them: "He who has ears to hear, let him hear." Well, we basically all have ears, but the Lord obviously knows that we don't all use them.

Some of us hear what we want to hear, right? In Acts 7:57 the people did not want to hear Stephen's sermon, so they stopped up their ears. While most adults don't plug their ears with their fingers in public, we might as well for the good our ears are doing us.

"If you have ears," to paraphrase Jesus, "use them!" The very first place we must turn our ears to is the Word of God. Have you ever turned your child's face to you and said, "Listen to me! I'm trying to save you from a lot of trouble." God's word does the same, saving us from hell to be exact, if we will only listen.

Beyond that, it's key to relationships to listen to one another. Good listening is *not*:

- Looking at the person while being lost in your own world.
- Interrupting the person.
- Changing the subject.
- Formulating what you are going to say next while he is talking.
- Listening for the sake of winning your own argument.
- Jumping to conclusions about what he really means.
- Assuming you already know what he is going to say anyway.
- Rolling your eyes.

Good listening *is*:

- Looking at the person when possible.
- Tuning out distractions when possible.
- Paying close attention to gestures and nonverbal clues.
- Clarifying what was said.
- Affirming that what he said was significant.

Not every affirmation has to be, "Yes, I agree," or "Wow! That was powerful," but laughing at a joke or asking further questions about what is being said communicates to the talker that what he is saying is significant.

James 1:19 says, "So then, my beloved brethren, let every man be swift to hear, slow to speak, slow to wrath." A relationship therapist couldn't give any better advice.

Tempted to Nag? Be Quiet!

What is the biggest reason to eliminate nagging from your communication core? It doesn't work! In fact, it achieves the opposite of what is intended. If I turned on the six o'clock news and I found the same top story, followed by the same local news, sports, and weather night after night after night, I would become quite weary. In fact, on the second night, I would turn it off. Wives who continually ask their husbands to do the same undone chore or wish out loud over and over again that he would just quit some annoying habit achieve the same success of an old news program. You can keep nagging if you want, but you should know that, after the second night, you've probably been tuned out.

Proverbs 27:15 says that the nag is like a continual drip on a rainy day. Is that really how you want to be perceived by your husband? None of us are perfect, and in an ideal Godly relationship, both the husband and wife can accept that fact. Evaluate the behavior you would like changed in your spouse. Is it something that deeply hurts or concerns you? If not, let it go. If you feel the behavior does need to be addressed and is causing resentment to build in you, then ask him if he would be willing to sit down and talk. Use good listening skills during the talk, and balance your request with loads of encouragement—build him up—and appreciation. Tell him the specific ways he makes you happy.

In a Christian marriage, if your husband is willing, it's a good idea to have scheduled one-on-one talk slots several times a week for 20 to 30 minutes alone and uninterrupted. Keep the tone in these positive, ideally including prayer, and they will get better and better. Then if there is something you need to work out, this scheduled time will provide a time to air it.

In some marriages the husband may not be cooperative enough to agree to "talk time." Even so, any nagging should be avoided because it will only continue to wedge an emotional separation. Instead, use every opportunity you can find to communicate thanks and praise, and it may be that your husband will have a greater desire to please you on his own.

Threatening, to Get Your Way? Be Quiet!

This is not just for wives. While it's true that a married woman may threaten to withhold sex or even domestic responsibilities unless she gets her way, this kind of behavior is not limited to the marital context. I heard a woman tell an eldership that, until they changed their service times, she would be going somewhere else. At one congregation, there were too many cookies at vacation Bible school. Since one of the ladies was not consulted before the cookies were bought, she threatened not to help in the kitchen the next year. I'm not making this up!

These women were not displaying a meek and quiet spirit. A meek and quiet spirit really doesn't even have a "my way." This spirit desires to do things God's way, and within that realm, bends and flexes to the convenience and plans of others whenever possible. It's really what submission is—not a popular idea in society, but nonetheless, God's idea. In marriage, a wife submits to her husband (Ephesians 5:22); in the church, the sheep submit to the shepherds (Hebrews 13:17); and in all other human affairs, we submit to one another: "Yes, all of you be submissive to one another, and be clothed with humility, for 'God resists the proud, but gives grace to the humble'" (1 Peter 5:5).

Ready to Discourage Someone? Be Quiet!

Encouragement, building one another up, is absolutely essential for the church to thrive. Why else would the first churches be reminded so many times to exhort and edify?

Why was the nation of Israel doomed to wander aimlessly for forty years instead of immediately conquering and taking possession of the prize? It was a direct result of discouragers. There was just a handful—ten among a nation of millions. But their discouragement spread like flu, and their words, "We are not able to go up against the people, for they are stronger than we" (Numbers 13:31), made the hearts of the people melt (Joshua 14:8).

What's the discourager saying? "God isn't big enough."

Words can do that. Sometimes the spirit of Eeyore floods our church buildings. It's just hard to remain enthusiastic when there's a discourager in your midst. She is the one who says, "We've tried that before and it doesn't work." She says, "We just can't grow." Once I heard her say to an excited newcomer, "You just come for the door knocking and find out for yourself. You'll see it doesn't work." What she's really saying between the lines is what the ten spies said: "God isn't big enough."

God couldn't be more displeased. This story of conquering Canaan is not so much one of weapons and tactics as one of attitude. Six times in the first chapter of Joshua, God personally encouraged Joshua: "Only be strong and of good courage." In His last instructions to Moses, He made sure of one thing: "But charge Joshua, and encourage him, and strengthen him" (Deuteronomy 3:28).

A few words of encouragement or discouragement can have a domino effect for many generations. How many times have you heard an adult reflect on something he was told as a child by someone who is now dead? In your circle of acquaintances, I bet you know multiple people named Joshua or Caleb. I further wager you don't know any named Gaddiel, Palti, Oshea, or Igal. It was Caleb who said, "Let us go up at once and possess it, for we are well able to overcome it." Thousands of years later, it is his echo of encouragement we want instilled in our children from the time we name them. God himself speaks of the "spirit" of Caleb being different (Numbers 14:24). A meek and quiet spirit is like that. It's different. When the odds are stacked against us, a meek and quiet spirit can gently knock over the stack. Spoken meekness says we can because God can.

Ready to Complain? Be Quiet!

The more I read the scriptures, the more I find that the "little" sins, the ones we overlook and laugh about, are huge. Preachers are not usually fired for complaining and people rarely ask for prayers to help them overcome the sin of ingratitude. It's a part of American culture. If we don't like the weather, we say so, and if our french fries aren't greasy enough, we take them back to the counter. It may be part of our culture, but we're not really about that culture, are we? If we are in the body of Christ, then we are called out of the world.

To God, complaining and ingratitude are not so little; they're huge. "Well, sure," you might say, "it's big when it's about big things like marriage or children, the church or its leadership." How about food? Is it a big deal to complain about what's on your plate? It's about big enough to cause the Lord's anger to be aroused to the point of sending a plague so horrible that before the eaters could even finish chewing, they were both burying and being buried (Numbers 11:6, 33–34). In a list of ungodly behaviors in 2 Timothy 3:2–4, see how "unthankful" ranks. Next time you start to say, "I wonder if it's ever going to rain again" or "I wonder if it's ever going to stop raining" or "sandwiches again?", bite your tongue. It's a big deal. A meek and quiet spirit can't complain.

Quit Interrupting and Disrupting

"Please, let me tell just one lie," Mama said. It could have more directly been worded, "Quit interrupting." I was not only interrupting, but I was also disrupting. A woman who lacks a meek and quiet spirit does both. She interrupts progress by criticizing and discouraging. She disrupts harmony by butting in or spreading gossip. The salvation of many can hinge on the very presence or absence of one meek and quiet spirit.

And who said the role of women was insignificant?

Put your hand over your mouth.

—Job 21:5

Something for <u>YOU</u> to Do . . .

1. Think about the 40 years God's people spent in the wilderness after the spies' report. What calamities would have never happened during that period of wandering if the Israelites had been encouraged to take possession immediately by the spies?

2. In what specific ways within the church do we bend and flex for the sake of harmony?

3. Who is submission for? What percentage of your life would you say is spent in submission while what percentage is spent with others submitting to you? How does this fit in with 1 Peter 5:5?

4. Is it easier for us to praise some people more than others? And is expressing praise more natural for some of us? Why do you think this is?

5. For the married, approach your husband, if he is approachable, about a 20 to 30 minute slot three days a week for "talk time." Early mornings work well for some couples and can be accompanied by a walk if you both are game. Don't approach him with the attitude of "you don't have time for me," but with the attitude of "I love to spend time with you."

6. How many times does Leviticus 19 include the phrase "I am the Lord"? Why?

7. What immature threats can you think of that can or have occurred within the home? Within the church?

8. Who was the meekest man ever to live, according to scripture? List some of his characteristics. Are these the same characteristics that are valued by God in a woman?

9. When you are talking to someone, what communicates to you that she is not listening?

10. What does the critical person miss? What does the critical parent miss? What kinds of things can we miss in our spiritual family if we are critical?

~ Spark Plugs ~

And speaking of french fries · · ·

Did anyone else catch the article about the french fry that sold for $202.50 on eBay? This was a lone fry, *part* of a potato. I like my carbs but this is ridiculous. I once paid $4.50 for an order of fries at the airport and haven't gotten over it yet.

Do you realize that the street value of a single fry is not even peanuts but peanut hulls? Because I'm a serious journalist, I insisted on researching this topic firsthand by immediately driving to my neighborhood Mickey D's to place an order. The cost was one dollar before tax, and there were exactly 56 fries in the pouch. Do the math and you come up with 1.8 cents per fry?

Not only this, but according to the article, the french fry was put up for auction June 24 and actually sold July 2. Call me picky, but I like mine hot.

On further research, I learned that the french fry eBay site had over 19,000 hits which leaves me wondering how many complete lunatics may be walking around out there at any given time, and just who might be in the booth next to you at the fast food place. It brought several words to mind like e-crazy, e-food poison, e-bankruptcy and e-nough is e-nough.

It also left me wondering what other items were bringing this kind of price. Should I start going through my garbage taking digital pictures of totally worthless items in the hopes of finding thousands of idiots looking to waste $200? It sounded plausible so I did some more research. Two three-cent stamps had a winning bid of $265.50, and something described as a "lot of bone, underwear, and old shoe buttons" had a bid of $5.00. So, I thought, I would not have to actually sort through my garbage, but could just sell it by the scoop.

The high bidder for the "lot," by the way, was "im-a_kingskid3" which explains why he has money to blow on bone, underwear, and old shoe buttons while the rest of us are buying milk and eggs.

But back to the french fry. When I read the whole article I learned that this wasn't just an ordinary fry but was claimed to be the world's largest french fry. It was bound to happen sooner or later because in my vast experience of world traveling—Natchez, Mississippi, and back—I have found billboards for literally everything from the world's largest flea market to the world's largest flea. There are usually at least three fireworks stands at any given exit, each of which is the world's largest. I have personally used the world's largest restroom and eaten six inches of the world's largest beef jerky.

So we have desperadoes vying for a chance to be famous by having a 6.75-inch french fry stashed in their freezer. (Which in my opinion is not colossal. My college roommate had a toenail longer than that!) That's what eBay is all about. It's changed the image of auction if auction ever had it. Watching old black-and-white movies when I was young, I got the idea that an auction was a place where a lot of people who all looked like David Niven sat around in suits with handkerchiefs emerging from their breast pockets and did the queen's wave whenever someone held up an item (usually Mona Lisa) and asked who would give a million dollars.

The price gave my husband lockjaw in an open position.

Later, my dad drastically altered my image of auctions by taking me to a car auction in Cullman, Alabama. No suits. No queen's waves. Just a lot of badly dented vehicles (one of them driven in backward because it would only go in reverse) coming through a garage with doors at both ends, and a guy with a microphone singing "Ya Pa Betty Botter Butter Ding Ping Ting Da Money" to the tune of *Folsom Prison Blues*. I was in culture shock for days.

Then shortly after marriage, my husband and I caught antique fever, because as of yet no one has discovered a vaccine for that. We went to an estate auction which is a place where human vultures gather to grab up all the good stuff a person leaves behind when he dies. I *really* wanted the lead crystal pedestal punch bowl, but ended up with the canister vacuum and a thingy from the barn that might have once been part of the outhouse, but had been chewed on by a famous horse. The price gave my husband lockjaw in an open position.

Now there's eBay. It's different because you can agonize over the item for up to 14 days instead of 30 seconds. You can go online to search for a Snow Village and end up bidding on a 50 percent off coupon for Snow

Pea Sushi Bar in Texas. You can set your alarm for 3:32:15 a.m. because you want to beat out the guy from Hong Kong at the last second only to find out your Internet server is down. You can call your brother at 3:32:54 a.m. and beg him to get up and bid for you, reminding him of the time he overstretched your Slinky.

EBay. Who knew? A business that started because the founder's wife wanted to exchange Pez dispensers with other collectors. Who knew it could grow to an auction house where anyone in the world could have an opportunity to invest in something this huge? 6.75 inches of french fry.

I think the lesson we should learn from all of this is obvious. Never eat out without a tape measure.

Johnnia (left) with college chum, Jacksonville, Alabama, late 1940s.

Top: Johnnia (right) with friend at school (c. 1944).

Middle: Johnnia, age 3.

Bottom: Lois Elliott Duncan and Johnnia, 1954.

CHAPTER 6

LET MARGIE GET HER SOME FIRST

Selflessness

Love . . . does not seek its own.

—I Corinthians 13:4–5

· · · · · · · · · · · · · · · ✤ · ✤ · · · · · · · · · · · · · · ·

If you say something like "pass the okra" at the dinner table, usually the mom will pass you the okra. Not at ours.

Somewhere, generations ago (no one alive knows exactly when), there was a lady named Margie who apparently frequented one of my ancestor's dining rooms. No one knows what she looked like, whether or not she was really related to us, or if she liked okra. Of all the great things she may have done in her lifetime, only one is remembered. Margie, when asked to pass the okra or the peas or the butter or the syrup, evidently without fail said, "Let me get me some first."

So if you come to my house—or to the house of one of my siblings or even distant cousins—and you wish to partake of the okra, do not say "pass the okra" intending to have the okra passed to you in any kind of immediate fashion. Even though my mama had the feet of great gospel preachers under her table from time to time, the okra passing was not expedited, because Mama knew and handed down that the correct response to "pass the okra" is to pick up the okra, begin serving yourself, and say, "Let Margie get her some first."

• •

Mama's words in this case are not particularly wise or pithy, but they do make a great starting place—for a subject that is. "Let Margie get her some first" is fun among friends and guests at the supper table, but the notion of serving self before all others has become a hallmark of the current generation.

The Virtue of Selfishness

Almost a half century ago, Ayn Rand wrote a book titled *The Virtue of Selfishness.*[1] While most would not outright call it a virtue, society has been infiltrated with the doctrine of selfishness:

- "Look out for number one, because no one else is going to"

- "Learning to love yourself is the greatest love of all"

- "Put yourself first for a change"

- "It's my turn."

It has become the theme of advice in morning shows and talk TV. Professionals are putting on seminars throughout the nation teaching us how to put ourselves first as if we haven't known how since the time we screamed for a bottle.

Even love, we are told, should be selfish. Columnist Gary Hull put it this way:

---

1 Ayn Rand, *The Vvirtue of Selfishness* (New York: Signet, 1964).

The perverse view of love [is] entailed in the belief that it is self-sacrificial. Genuine love is the exact opposite. It is the most selfish experience possible, in the true sense of the term: it benefits your life in a way that involves no sacrifice of others to yourself or of yourself to others. To love a person is selfish because it means that you value that particular person, that he or she makes your life better, that he or she is an intense source of joy—to you (Australia's *Herald Sun*, February 2, 2004; *Louisville Courier-Journal*, February 13, 2005).

Whose view is perverse? Hull's idea is that I love someone else because it ultimately brings pleasure back to me, but Hull's idea is way wide of the mark.

I do love chocolate for this reason, and homemade rolls. And many of the people I love so deeply bring a great deal of pleasure to me. But beyond that, I love them even when they bring sorrow and hardship. Biblical love is unselfish at the core. "But God demonstrates His own love toward us, in that while we were still sinners, Christ died for us" (Romans 5:8). Exactly where is the pleasure in experiencing agonizing pain and death while those you love are slapping you and spitting in your face?

The problem with the doctrine of self first is not only its root negligence of compassion and benevolence toward the other guy, but if we have put self first, then God is necessarily also somewhere else on the list, until eventually He is not on the list at all. Rand, in her blatant selfishness doctrine, attributed Thanksgiving as a day we celebrate what we have earned. Recently Debi Ghate, Vice President of Academic Programs at the Ayn Rand Institute, expounded on her mockery, saying:

It's no accident that Americans have a holiday called Thanksgiving—a yearly tradition when we pause to appreciate the "bountiful harvest" we've reaped. What is today's version of the "bountiful harvest"? It's the affluence and success we've gained. It's the cars, houses, and vacations we enjoy. It's the life-saving medicines we rely on, the stock portfolios we build, the beautiful clothes we buy and the safe, clean streets we live on. It's the good life. How did we get this "bountiful harvest"? Ask any hard-working American; it sure wasn't by the "grace of God." It didn't grow on a fabled "money tree." *We created it* by working hard, by desiring the best money can buy . . . (*San Francisco Chronicle*, November 23, 2006).

According to Their Own Desires

Putting self first eventually involves putting God nowhere, and yet I continue to see the idea sold to us, women and moms in particular, to the degree that we now are supposed to experience guilt if we do sacrifice for our kids or if we do put others' needs above our own.

Satan would have us swallow this advice whole, but he knows we are not going to take any advice that we know comes from him. Satan works counsel in attractive packages. Rehoboam took the advice of young peers who promised a selfish success. I doubt if Rehoboam would have even considered their message if they had been dressed in an evil garb, announced as bringing Satan's message. Neither would we, but TV anchors have a white toothy smile and invite as guests sharply dressed psychologists who promise that same selfish success. They seem genuinely to care.

Now think about it: Does someone who promotes the doctrine of "put yourself first" and "look out for number one" really have an agenda to help me? It's a paradox. How about someone who gave up everything including His own life to help me? Would that Person genuinely care? Could I listen to His advice? Here it is: "Therefore, whatever you want men to do to you, do also to them" (Matthew 7:12).

How then can the doctrine of self-first, so averse to Jesus' teaching, become so accepted as a good thing, even among religious people? Here's the answer.

> For the time will come when they will not endure sound doctrine, but according to their own desires, because they have itching ears, they will heap up for themselves teachers; and they will turn their ears away from the truth, and be turned aside to fables (2 Timothy 4:3–4).

"According to their own desires" indicates complete selfishness. Selfishness breeds fables. Fables are enjoyable. In fables, dogs talk and chickens wear tuxedos. But what we know about fables is that they can't really happen. Selfishness cannot be a virtue; that's a fable.

The Virtue of Self-Denial

Women are told over and over, "You are just going to have to learn how to say no." Interestingly, Jesus has this to say:

> If anyone wants to sue you and take away your tunic, let him have your cloak also. And whoever compels you to go one mile, go with him two.

Give to him who asks you, and from him who wants to borrow from you do not turn away (Matthew 5:40-42).

It doesn't sound like Jesus is telling us, "You're going to have to learn to say no." It sounds like Jesus is saying, "You're going to have to learn to say yes."

It's true that we do have to be able to say no at times in order to say yes. We may have to say no to the PTA in order to say yes to lodging a stranger. We may have to say no to coaching little league in order to say yes to sitting up with the critically ill. These are life choices for which we are not going to find specific scriptural precedence. What we do find are guiding principles which can help us determine the right decision. Jesus has given us direction for helping the poor, the hungry, the prisoner, and the sick (Matthew 25:34–46). He has also strongly warned us against building resentment in our children (Mark 9:42).

Putting self first eventually involves putting God nowhere.

So we have this responsibility to help others; also, we have a responsibility to focus on our own families. And we are to do all this while seeking first His kingdom (Matthew 6:33). These are principles which help us decide which activities go in the "yes" column and which in the "no" at the time.

"Whosoever will come after me, let him deny himself" (Mark 8:34 KJV). The only person I am told that I consistently need to say "no" to is myself.

Take Time

Does this mean we are barred from doing anything enjoyable or relaxing? We were created to need rest and nourishment. On the seventh day, after an unfathomable six days of the most powerful and perfect work ever, God wasn't so busy, was He? After single-handedly taking care of the physical hunger of over five thousand people, Jesus went to the mountain to be alone (John 6). I believe women, moms of preschoolers in particular, should follow His lead. Did you ever notice when the mother bird flies from the nest to find the worm for her little ones, they are not tagging along behind her in the sky? Shouldn't the human mother be allowed the same worm-hunting privilege as the bird mother? Just a couple of hours alone once a week can turn even a grocery store into a peaceful island of solitude. More important, a woman must reserve time to be alone and commune with her God. On most occasions when we find Jesus seeking recluse, this was the reason.

For both sanity and fidelity to prevail, a married woman must take time for her husband. This includes bedroom and non-bedroom time. Soon after we had moved to a new town, unfamiliar territory for both of us, I remember waving to my husband three different times as we passed each other in different vehicles, each searching for different soccer fields. I remember thinking, "I've got to meet this guy in person!" Don't make him last on your to-do list.

Notice I keep suggesting to "take" time or "reserve" time, instead of "find" time. So many times, people say, "I've got to find time to read my Bible" or "find the time to be with my husband." Good luck with that. Some people find four-leaf clovers, but it's not likely.

How does fulfilling this need to be alone with those important to you, including your God, reconcile with denying yourself? Perfectly. Isn't it interesting that God's directives to sacrifice in the Old Testament usually required a journey apart from the business of everyday life? Similarly, saying no to something on your busy calendar can be a sacrifice leading you to a journey apart with your children, your husband, or your God.

The Virtue of Service

When we talk about virtuous people, we seldom begin to list all the things they have done for themselves. Can you just imagine if Dorcas had done all the sewing for herself instead of others? I'll wager that no one would have been holding up the garments remembering all the things she had made for herself.

The "let Margie get her some first" attitude is diametrically opposed to true Christianity. In John 13 there were quite a few Margies at the dinner table, only they were named things like John, Peter, and Andrew. The custom in the dry, dusty region in the first century was to have a person assigned to washing the bare feet of the guests before dinner. The Margies weren't particularly interested in this chore, and so taking some twenty-first century advice long before it's time, they decided to "look out for number one." They would eat first—think about feet later if at all. There was one among them, though, who had committed uncompromisingly to denying Himself. Though unarguably the most honorable dinner guest of all time, God Himself in the flesh, He laid aside His outer garment—"rolled up his sleeves" in our colloquial—took a basin of water, and began scrubbing away foot dirt. Those who believe that selfishness is a virtue must, in essence, believe that Christianity is not. The two simply cannot coexist.

Self or Savior—that is the ultimatum at the heart of discipleship. If there is any debate about this at all, Jesus has put it to rest with the following words that just can't get any clearer.

If anyone desires to be first, he shall be last of all and servant of all.
—Mark 9:35

The Virtue of Sacrifice

The components of self-denial are both service and sacrifice. Christ spent His earthly life serving, leading up to the ultimate sacrifice. We are to take up both of these qualities, according to Romans 12:1.

As Christian women, we opt for sacrifice in little decisions like passing okra and washing feet, and the importance of such acts cannot be minimized. But we also need to use the same standard for the biggies. Should moms sacrifice for little souls that enter their world in the prime of their careers?

One mom, who was presented an attractive job offer, explained to me, "This is a one-time opportunity for me. If I wait three years until my daughter is in school, this opportunity will be gone." She was probably right, but she was staring down at a rarer opportunity in training pants and golden curls. In three short years, the opportunity for weekdays spent with that toddler would be forever gone. Another career opportunity may or may not come again, but one thing is certain: those childhood years would never come again. The mom who spoke to me was an excellent candidate among several for the coveted job, but she was absolutely the only individual on the globe who could serve as mother to that little girl.

Sunday I listened briefly to a celebrity gossip show. The star being interviewed would soon have her life filmed on a reality show. When asked about her young daughter, she said, "She is a part of my life, but not the focus."

I understand that this comment was probably made concerning the filming of the show, not necessarily the life of those in the cast. However, isn't a reality show supposed to portray the true reality? I'm afraid it's a "reality" description of the way moms function, who have swallowed the "put self first" theology. Children are often like puppies or porch swings—a part of life that provides enjoyment when the owners have the time, but they are not the focus.

Materials by educated people who say that sacrifice is overrated and unnecessary may be soothing ointment for itching ears, but they violate the pattern put forth in God's Word. Don't even think about your own things, to paraphrase Paul in Philippians 2:4, but be concerned about the things of others. Again, Paul says in 1 Corinthians 10:33, "Not seeking my own profit, but the profit of many, that they may be saved."

God First

Though the decision process may be grueling at the time, I have never known of a person who made the choice to sacrifice who ever once regretted it. That's the beauty of doing it God's way. It's easy to pillow your head at night.

It just seems to me that if you pass the okra bowl around first, it almost never comes back to you empty. May we never forget: the remedy for a harried life is not in learning to put ourselves first; it's in learning to put God first.

*Let each of you look out not only for his own
interests, but also for the interests of others.*

—Philippians 2:4

Something for YOU to Do . . .

1. Read 1 Corinthians 13:4–8. List the attributes of love below. Circle the ones which are about bringing pleasure directly to self.

_____   _____   _____

_____   _____   _____

_____   _____   _____

_____   _____   _____

_____

2. Take 25! Deliberately squeeze a 25-minute unit out of your week. Stay up later one night; go to bed earlier; skip checking email, whatever it takes, and give it in additional sacrifice, whether directly in communion with

God or in service to others (in your household or not). Afterward, evaluate the efforts and the rewards.

3. How is spending time alone in line with Jesus' teaching? What is the difference in taking time "by yourself" and taking time "for yourself?"

4. Besides the ultimate sacrifice of the crucifixion, what other specific sacrifices and seemingly change of plans do we find in the life of Jesus?

5. One big decision, that of a mom to pursue her career or not, based on sacrifice was used in the text. What other big life decisions involve sacrifice?

6. On the flip side of the coin, what situations can cause a woman to choose employment as the sacrificial answer?

7. Listen and look this week. Where do you hear the message of self-service in our culture? Is it subtle or blatant?

8. Rehoboam's friends were not the only bad advisors in the scriptures. What other "Dear Abby's" gave advice to behave selfishly? What was the result?

9. Research the Ayn Rand Institute. Share your findings and tell whether or not you think it has influenced American culture.

Spark Plugs

And speaking of Thanksgiving . . .

It conjures memories of paper pilgrim hats, the smell of cider on the stove, wreaths on the door, and the living room brawl over whether the offensive line had a false start or was just stomping a few roaches on the field.

Fall magazines feature matching sweater families laughing in leaf piles bursting with color. Our Thanksgivings are different. They are spent a smidgen to the southeast in Calhoun County, and have, in general, consisted of a few rounds of the stomach viruses, a tableside discussion of hemorrhoid surgery, trips to the emergency room, and badly burned fudge. Along with the normal football stuff.

When 20 people gather around a table for 8, the fun begins. One of my fondest Thanksgiving memories was what we warmly refer to as "the see-saw episode" also known as the time Scotty got up from the long harvest-style bench, shifting the weight and sending the other 13 people rolling downward into Cindy (who was coincidentally holding the sweet potato casserole) causing her to engage in her own contact sport (better know as the rear-end-linoleum impact play) while still saving the casserole with only a half-cup splattered on her glasses, pilgrim earrings, and highly festive vest.

And from the living room, "*Touchdown!*"

The seating arrangement can get creative, as I remember numerous times when the ironing board lot fell to me. Then there are the decorations. We fondly reflect on Mom's yearly apple turkey with two toothpick legs and a third stuck in his bottom for balance. He was truly the perfect poster child for underprivileged turkeys everywhere.

For all the novelty of the seating and decor, the menu is often "noveler." Half of us stick staunchly to tradition. (What is that wobbly red stuff and does anyone ever eat any?) The other half wishes they had, especially when Veronica decided corned beef cabbage rolls were a nice alternative to turkey. Other cooking ventures lead to various remarks (these are real):

"How many times did you put sage in this dressing?"

"I think you got the vanilla mixed up with the mascara."

"Is this a potato or Swiss cheese?"

"I'm allergic to turkey this year."

And from the living room: "*Interception!*"

After the meal, we usually hate ourselves for eating that much pump-kin pie, for continuing to pick at the turkey after we had said it was the last time, and *who* got this many dishes dirty? Some years ago, we invented the cup game in order to save kitchen clean-up time. There is a number on the bottom of each cup, and the deal is you must keep your same cup all weekend instead of getting a clean cup every time you feel a sweet-tea urge. As an incentive, we have a drawing at the end of the weekend, and if your cup number is chosen, you could possibly win an emery board, silly putty, or other parting gifts. This worked well when there were 13 of us. As our number increased, we grew older, the setting became more chaotic, and we can no longer remember our names, much less our cup numbers. The theme for the weekend is cup confusion. It goes like this:

"I know I'm number 12. I think."

"I'm number 12. You must be 21. Turn it the other way."

"No. That was Labor Day."

"Is this a 6 or a 9?"

And from the living room: "*It's good! 49!*"

We remind ourselves to order pizza next year, eat off paper towels, and drink from the water hose. After a massive clean-up maneuver, we secretly hide all the sale papers from Sami who has a tendency to knock on our bedroom doors at 4:15 a.m. and whisper, "Is anyone going with me to the After-Thanksgiving-Day Sale?"

I, for one, have done this one too many times. Last year, it was a mere 17 degrees, and she decides, for some completely unknown reason, to roll the window down on my van, at which point it gets stuck. There is noth-ing quite like driving through the countryside in your pajamas to your nearby saving place (nearby meaning 32 miles) with a 17-degree breeze blowing through your hair at 4:15 a.m.—*that's in the morning!*

In the midst of this just off-center family, I am thankful. Thankful for 1:00 a.m. laughter, for little towel-caped crusaders rounding the corner to rescue the turkey, for giant hugs and gentle tears, for shelter, soldiers, seasons . . .

And from the living room, "*Safety!*"

Top: Johnnia, early twenties.

Middle: Johnnia holding first baby, John.

Bottom: School chums, early 1940s. Johnnia on far right.

PRAY FOR GETTIN' SOMEWHERE AND SITTIN' DOWN

Peace Amid Chaos

The peace of God, which surpasses all understanding, will guard your hearts and minds through Christ Jesus.

—Philippians 4:7

With four kids, life is never a vacuum. It's more like a vacuum cleaner: one that is very loud, with three wheels instead of four, and a hole in the bag. When the four of us were scurrying around Mama's feet, there must have been an avalanche of questions: What time is it? Is this a tick? Why does she get to lick the bowl and I don't? Why are there little trees on my plate? Is there supposed to be syrup in my toy box?

My mama stayed on the quiz show as long as she could most days. I know it was difficult with all the distractions. We also had a lot of celebrities in our small den. Batman really could suspend himself from the light fixture while Orville and Wilbur Wright taped wings to the salt shaker and Cher screamed into the hairbrush.

Sometimes as the questions abounded, a glazed look came over Mama's face, and she must have answered, "Just get somewhere and sit down."

She must have answered that way then, but by the time I can remember her words, they had changed a little. Apparently, she had deferred to the phrase so frequently that as my older brother was praying for this and that, he threw in "and pray for gettin' somewhere and sittin' down."

Forever after that, amid the chaos of frantic activity, Mama would lift my chin with her finger and say, "Pray for gettin' somewhere and sittin' down."

May we all pray the same.

● ●

I find that most women are Marthas by nature. We are troubled about much (Luke 10:41). If Martha could have taken two steps back from her kitchen and viewed the scene objectively, she might have laughed. There was, in reality, nothing to be upset about. Everyone was healthy; there was a roof overhead; no catastrophe was pending. It was an extraordinarily good day. She was among family, she was blessed with food to prepare, and the Lord Himself was in very near proximity.

Martha could not see the blatant blessings for the trivial frustrations. Mary could not see the trivial frustrations for the blatant blessings. Mary got somewhere and sat down. Martha should have prayed to do the same.

Preoccupied with Preparation

Of all the powerful stories included in the scriptures, could there possibly be a more relevant one?

If your congregation operates like mine, dedicated Martha's are juning around in the kitchen every time the doors are open. Thank God for their constant ministry. Jesus himself provided a fellowship meal to a huge assembly at least twice (Matthew 14–15). The night of His arrest and looming death, He chose to share a meaningful meal with those closest to Him (John 13). On the last occasion Jesus found His disciples after the resurrection, His first words to them were, "Children, have you any food?" (John 21:5). Our church basements and kitchens have been the hub of spiritual activity refreshing missionaries, launching work programs, feeding the homeless, and getting one step nearer in sharing the gospel with that contact every time his feet slide under the folding table.

Sometimes, though, we get so preoccupied with the preparation that we forget the occasion. The occasion that Martha forgot was that her Lord was in close proximity with a wealth of spiritual wisdom for those who would get somewhere and sit down. "Martha was distracted with much serving" (Luke 10:40). As the Lord's people, we have many occasions planned by our leadership to give us a wealth of spiritual wisdom. They come in the form of ladies' days, workshops, and special emphasis Sundays. And they inevitably include a meal. What we forget is that the word *include* does not mean "revolve around." If someone asked us the reason for the occasion, surely none of us would answer "to eat"—not physically anyway.

Get Somewhere and Sit Down

It was the same in Martha's case, but she became so encumbered with her "food chairman" responsibilities that she missed the whole thrust of the occasion. Last Sunday morning, kitchen workers were stirring and covering and plugging in and preheating to beat sixty. As I turned the burner down to simmer and headed upstairs for worship, one of the workers said, "I hope they tape the service, because I don't think I can make it."

"Come on, Martha [not her real name]," I joked, "You can make it. I'm coming up myself." Together that day, we soaked in a wealth of profitable Bible teaching. Later I thought, "I can't believe we could have missed out on that just to stir some beans." The pots and the pans were calling, but I'm so glad we opted for getting somewhere and sitting down.

Martha's frenzied kitchen manners turned what should have been a happy occasion completely upside down. How many times have we done the same? Martha was the one who welcomed Him into her house (Luke 10:39). If the story had ended there, Martha would have been exemplary in the realm of hospitality. As the dinner hour neared, she simply stressed herself out. I don't know if she ran out of flour or the bread stuck to the pan, but the little things evidently built up until hospitality quickly turned to throwing her hands in the air, storming out of the kitchen, accusing her sister of laziness, and demanding that the Lord take sides. What Martha had intended as a good thing, an opportunity to visit with and refresh her friend and Lord, she turned into a highly tense situation. Can you just imagine that whoever was present at the time was just a wee bit uncomfortable? Nobody was really having fun at that moment.

A Tone of Peace

Some years ago, bumper stickers and T-shirts proclaimed: "If Mama ain't happy, ain't nobody happy." It's true, isn't it? As women, we set the tone for the occasion, even if there technically isn't one. We have a knack for turning the best laid plans for hospitality into sheer last minute panic. Who's happy then?

If we're generally responsible for the tone, hallelujah! We have control of whether this is going to be a good time or a bad time. Ultimately, that may depend on whether we "pray for gettin' somewhere and sittin' down."

When you feel pulled in every direction as Martha must have that day, here are a few suggestions.

1. *Pray.* Maybe that's what Martha was doing. She addressed the Lord directly, but I'm not talking about that kind of prayer. Walk away calmly while you can, close a door, and spend three minutes of grateful solitude with the One who cares the most. Pull over if you need to, get out of the noisy car, and rest just a minute while talking to your Lord. I'd rather arrive somewhere five minutes late and relaxed, than five minutes early in the "Martha" state.

2. *Sing.* We all have favorite hymns we know by heart. Whatever yours are, sing out. You might have messes, but it will lessen the stresses.

3. *Laugh.* Find the humor; it's usually there. A caterer recently was running late for the first in a series of delivery stops. When he got his car loaded, it wouldn't start. After several attempts, he decided to move all the boxes to his other vehicle. As Murphy's Law would have it, he picked up a large box full of tiny round Christmas balls, the bottom fell out of the box, and hundreds of the candy balls rolled over his driveway and into the yard. "Travis, what did you do?" I asked when he was recounting this. His answer was, "I knew we could either laugh or cry, so I said, 'Let's laugh.'" How many "Martha" outbursts could be saved if we could locate that funny bone? It's a medical fact that it reduces the stress that will eventually otherwise be expressed in other ways.

4. *Hug.* The phrase "I need a hug" is not an empty one. Put your distractions aside for just a moment, and hug that child that is about to send you over the edge.

5. *Count.* I don't mean count to ten as most psychologists tell us. I mean count the roof overhead, the child at your feet, the food in the pantry, the fan in the window. Your blessings will always outnumber your messes.

6. *Reflect.* In the midst of your mayhem, find reflection. Think of the person you know who has gone through the unthinkable. Suddenly you will be glad to sweep up broken glass or a thousand Cheerios.

All these suggestions to take care of the small moments are based on the assumption that we have already done the big ones. We have internalized the scriptures on a regular, scheduled basis, and have visited with God one-on-one each day. We have got somewhere and sat down.

> *Now after six days Jesus took Peter, James, and John, and led them up on a high mountain apart by themselves.*
> —Mark 9:2

Lord, Do You Not Care?

Turbulent surroundings can build in us the thought that we are the only one putting forth any effort and nobody else even cares. "Lord, do you not care?" Martha said (Luke 10:40). She echoed the words of the apostles in Mark 4—another situation of turbulence. The boat was rocking, the waves were crashing, the storm was building, the apostles were panicking, and the Savior was sleeping. He had opted to get somewhere and sit down. And then came the words, "Teacher, do you not care?" (v. 38).

Jesus arose, rebuked the winds, and simply said, "Peace, be still" and there was a great calm (v. 39). A great calm. Isn't that what we need in our lives? Couldn't each Martha use a dose of that?

Does it take a storm of that magnitude to make us get somewhere and sit down? I'll bet there were some men on that boat who had some moments of deep reflection shortly thereafter. I think some loved ones got an extra long hug when the boat anchored that night.

Martha got bent out of shape over something so minute that it caused Jesus to shake His head, saying "Martha, Martha." Yet in the real storm of life, Martha got some perspective.

In John 11, immersed in the grief of a loved one, Martha wasn't ranting that no one cared, but was solidly relying on the truth that Christ was the Son of God, and that He was able "even now," even in this emotionally distressing time, to do whatever He asked of God. She had learned the value of prayer. She went secretly to get her sister and said, "The teacher has come and is calling for you." What a contrast in the meek behavior now and the frenzied fury then.

Are you running around in circles? Are you throwing your hands up? Will no one help you? Don't forget, the Lord is in the same place now that He was that day at Martha's; He's in the same place He was when the boat was rocking—He's in very close proximity. "Peace, be still," He says. And suddenly there is a great calm.

Pray for gettin' somewhere and sittin' down.

Be still, and know that I am God.

—Psalm 46:10

Something for <u>YOU</u> to Do . . .

1. Set a timer for two minutes and start writing your blessings below. I'll bet you can go nonstop without picking up the pen until the time ends.

2. The "Martha and Mary" story recurs constantly in the church. Think of specific examples when we stay in the kitchen instead of sitting at the feet of Jesus? How can we remedy this so we can "choose the better part" while still providing hospitality?

3. How important is the "fellowship meal"? Is there something about this physical gathering that enhances the spiritual ones? List other times besides the ones mentioned when Jesus was involved in a group meal. In each case, decide whether there was a benefit from this meal other than physical nourishment.

4. Have you ever been served by a harried little red hen? How does this contrast with the person who takes time to talk, laugh, and relax with you?

5. Does getting stressed out about time factors actually expedite your tasks? Come up with suggestions for handling these time-pressure moments more efficiently and effectively.

⌇ Spark Plugs ⌇

And speaking of quiz shows . . .

I used to be pretty good at them, if I do say so myself. That was during the rerun season and no one else in the den knew that I had secretly seen it before. So I would sit there quite calmly and say: "Who is navigator Bartholomeu Dias?" "The answer is A: gerontologist. Final." "Guess a Q. It's obviously 'wedding ring quilt'"; and "Guess 28. The back half of the car is under 28!"

I amazed my peers and cat. This doesn't work anymore because by the time they show the rerun now, I can't remember the answers or the questions, but only have a slight blur that I might have seen that cashmere sweater before.

We are a game show family when we have the time. We know all the do's to the Jeopardy tune, "do-do-do-do-do-do-do . . ." We know the tune, yes, but we are pretty perplexed by the questions—I mean answers.

So on an answer like, "This book, published in 1833 by Alexis de Tocqueville, followed his nine-month visit to America," we all collectively know that the question is "Oh, oh, um, I should know this (snap your fingers) oh, what is it?" followed by someone buzzing in on the show with the correct answer, to which we all react, "Ooooh yeeeeah!"

Our game show enthusiasm spills over into other areas of life, where picking a restaurant goes like this, "A. Burger King, Fi-; No wait, C. Taco Bell is looking more and more like the right answer, but something says I should look at Ed's Pizza – I think I need to phone a friend." Then when we get there, my son points to a burger on the menu and says, "I'll make it a true daily double."

> The quiz show, in effect, didn't even have a quiz.

Every time a family member has a dumb look on his face when he's the last one to get a clue about what's going on, he meets with the remark, "Did you forget it was a prize puzzle?" My daughter turns into a Barker's Beauty at the grocery store, holding Choco-Crunchies and waving her hand around the box. And the spelling bee elimination was too quick. "What? No lifelines?" she muttered as she took her seat.

Isn't it weird that in Jeopardy, they go through about a million questions in a show, but the night-time prime time game show people only have to answer like three? They have learned the value of tension-building. The whole show is based, not on whether you actually know the answer to the question, but if in reality, you really want to see the question or not. "Ooooh, should I look at the question?" They turn to the audience for desperate help. They ask a panel of all-too-undecided significant others. And then finally, their great-grandmother is flown in from a nursing home on the coast to advise them whether they should look at the question or not.

In the end, everyone gets so involved in the emotional climax that they hardly realize that the quiz show, in effect, didn't even have a quiz.

So in the old days, you were up against the clock trying to answer as many questions as possible in a short amount of time. You could possibly win five thousand dollars. Now the object is to answer the least amount of questions while becoming a nervous wreck in front of your family and all of America as the music is mounting, and you get a million. And the show takes twice as long! It's disheartening at the end to realize you have literally spent a full hour of your life in which nothing more has happened than a contestant slammed a box three times.

I'm glad to see the swing toward cash prizes. I used to fear that some day I might end up on a game show, and horror of horrors, actually win something. Because in game shows, they had fabulous prizes like a statue of a banana pepper valued at thousands of dollars or a very large juke box or a trip to somewhere that people were swimming the ocean in order to get out of.

So when thinking about game shows, it's important to remember three things. First of all, remember it's just a game. If you end up having to say that you're dumber than a basset hound, life will go on.

Second, it's just a show. You can yell, "Take the money. I said take the money! What are you thinking? That's 47 house payments!" And the truth is that the contestant is not really ignoring you because she simply cannot hear you. This was taped months ago. It's a show!

And third remember . . . to have your pet spayed or neutered.

Johnnia working
in the kitchen (c. 1958).

Top: Johnnia and Lee with grandson Abel, 1991.

Bottom: Johnnia, age 8, proud of Shirley Temple doll.

CHAPTER 8

MORE MONEY THAN SENSE

Materialism

*I will do this: I will pull down my barns and build greater,
and there I will store all my crops and my goods.*

—Luke 12:18

There was nothing much more fun in those days than the amusement park once a summer and three hours away. You could fully soak your clothes and wallet, get nauseated, eat processed cartoon characters, get sunburned and watch highly talented otters all for the low, low price of a root canal.

As we walked along the scorching pavement, everyone else seemed to have more than we did—inflatable rattlesnakes, foam arrows sticking out of their temples, and neon Slurpees in alien bottles. But the best of all were the invisible dogs. There were quite a few of them sniffing around, I suppose, because there were a lot of people carrying around leashes which seemed to float in the air with nothing at all attached. I tried to kick one of the dogs once, but felt nothing.

I wanted a souvenir, too, but we knew from experience that our souvenirs came in the form of rocks and good sticks. Even I was not taken in by the invisible pooches. I whispered to Mama, "Why do you think all these people are spending money on something that isn't real?"

"Because," she said, "they have more money than sense."

• •

Most of us do, Mama. This is America, where we pay an 80-dollar fee and spend 175 dollars on equipment for a 4-year-old to play 8 games of a sport he doesn't understand. We throw away more food in a day than a Third World family sees in a month. We are compassionate enough to spend hundreds of dollars on surgery for a pet while we pray that the missionary will somehow get the funds needed to stay in the field. Could it be—could it be, Mama, that we have just a little more money than we do sense?

More Money than *Sense of Direction*

Some of us are born with it and some of us aren't. Usually, the "driving" half is the half that isn't born with it, and the "riding next to him in the front seat" half is the half who has plenty of it. Directions! Does anyone else wonder how the term "back seat driver" came along? Did wives used to ride around in the back seat? Don't we mean front seat, passenger side driver? Is it true that there are men who actually pay money for a device which has a woman's voice telling him where to turn? Can't you get those for free? Sort of? These are for people with more money than sense . . . of direction.

There was a Bible character—and yes, it was a man—who stopped and asked for directions: "What shall I do that I may inherit eternal life?" (Mark 10:17). He was trying to get to a specific place, and he needed direction to get there. It was the same place you and I are hopefully headed. The answers were simple and obvious enough. Don't cheat on your spouse; don't murder or steal; don't lie or cheat; honor your parents (v. 19). In short, be a good man.

Oh, and one more thing. "One thing you lack," Jesus said in verse 21, "Go your way, sell whatever you have and give to the poor, and you will have treasure in heaven; and come, take up the cross, and follow Me." It was here that he lost his sense of direction: "But he was sad at this word, and went away sorrowful, for he had great possessions" (v. 22). He simply had more money than sense.

A Fatal Turn

Was this an isolated case, or is it recorded three times in the Gospels for a reason? Is it possible that there is a whole breed of us without "walking around sense" because we have great possessions? What was the expression on Jesus' face when this good man who had approached him kneeling and asking for direction turned away, enslaved by a greater pull than eternal life? It was a grave moment because verse 21 says that Jesus loved him. Jesus' short commentary, as He watched him walk away, surprised His disciples. "How hard it is for those who have riches to enter the kingdom of God."

Is that about me? If you pillow your head tonight in a climate-controlled room and snuggle under covers on a comfortable mattress, it's about you. You have great possessions. You have money, but do you have more money than sense of direction? The money issue clouded the entire goal that the good man set out for. The story begins with his running toward, and ends with his walking from. Suddenly, he had lost his sense of direction, and the wrong turn was eternally fatal. It was the opposite direction of eternal life.

> We throw away more food in a day than a Third World family sees in a month.

The story was not a parable. He was and is as real as Peter, Andrew, Thomas, and the others standing around. What about those possessions that pulled him away? Where are they? He has been without them two thousand years longer than he was with them. Is there a single living heir who can hold them up in gratitude of the good man who protected them? Has there ever been a decision as foolish or regretted?

Only every day in America. Oh, we come running to Jesus each Sunday morning at nine. We are good men and women who don't cheat on our spouses or the IRS, but somewhere between Sundays, could it be that we lose direction? Is the pull of material things so great that we begin to forget the original destination? Master, what good thing can I do to inherit eternal life, that will not interfere with my retirement plan, my savings, my children's college funds, or our vacation? Have those become our destinations? Have we landed in the place of more money than sense . . . of direction?

More Money than *Sense of Decency*

How is it that more is less? The more material wealth we can accumulate, the lower the standard of morality deepens. How is it that in the midst of the Beverly Hills mansions, there is little sense of right or wrong, a stigma attached to claiming morals, and a stiff competition to make the tabloids for the latest immoral, illegal, or shocking escapade? How is it that the richest king in history had seven hundred wives and three hundred girlfriends on the side? (1 Kings 11:3). As more and more monetary wealth is acquired, it seems we have more money than sense . . . of decency.

It takes more to be average than it once did. When it comes to the middle class, somebody moved the middle, didn't they? The American dream has shifted from owning some property and building an A-frame house, working the land and feeding your family to having a house as big as everyone else's. Give us more bathrooms, more living space, more closet space, and more indoor saunas. We used to watch *The Brady Bunch* and dream that we, too, could have a house that big. Now we watch reruns and say, "Three kids in one bedroom? What are they thinking?"

Since 1973 the average living space in a new home has grown over 700 square feet.[1] It's like we've all added 7 rooms to our houses. What's happened morally during this material expansion? In 1970 there were 523,000 unmarried couples living together.[2] Now, the number is over six million.[3]

Hiking to the Outhouse

Somehow in our desire to acquire, we have lost our sense of decency. Mama would say we have lost our sense of shame. There's no shame in an unmarried couple living together. There's no shame in public drunkenness as long as you don't get caught driving that way. It's almost become an honor to be a celebrity with a prison sentence. Society is delighted by unwed fathers and mothers. As

1   "Construction Statistics", (National Association of Home Builders, 2008), http://www.nahb.org/page.aspx/category/sectionID=130 (accessed August 5, 2008).

2   Christine A. Bachrach. "Cohabitation and Reproductive Behavior in the U.S.," *Demography* 24, no. 4 (1987), http://www.jstor.org/pss/2061397 (accessed August 7, 2008

3   "Selected Social Characteristics in the United States: 2006", (U.S. Census Bureau, 2006), factfinder.census.gov/servlet/ADPTable? (accessed August 8, 2008).

a result, family relationships are temporary, and we have become more stunned and uncomfortable with foreclosure than with divorce.

What kid alive wouldn't give all the money in his piggy bank to have both a mama and a daddy in a loving, respectful environment under the same roof, even if it needs replacing? How is it that the adults are so confused? Because we have more money than sense. The standard is higher and the things we value are different. We're opting for multiple incomes, overtime, and higher salaries, but is it always to put bread on the table, and is anyone even sitting around the table that the bread is on? Is it sometimes to put more vehicles in the garage, more gadgets in the entertainment center, and a designer label on our backside? Does it have anything to do with the fact that American consumer debt, is now at 2.4 trillion dollars?[1]

The pull of material things is enough to cause us to buy things we can't really pay for. It's enough to pull Mama out of the home to try to make those payments. And as we spend less time with the family and more time in the workplace, in childcare institutions, and in front of the new entertainment gadgets, we begin to accept the decline in morals of the other pursuers. It's time to fix what's broken.

Sin is still sin, no matter how much money or how many bathrooms come with it. If it takes reverting to a simpler lifestyle to realize that sin is sin, may we all be hiking to the outhouse! It's interesting that the wealth of King Solomon was given to him by the Lord (1 Kings 3:13). Then Satan used that material blessing to ensnare him into sin and idolatry. Satan will always try to use the blessings we have from the Lord to turn us against Him. In far too many cases, he has met with success.

In our teen Bible classes, girls are honestly searching their hearts for answers to cultural dilemmas. Searching their hearts, yes—but have we failed to teach them to search also the scriptures? Many now can't see anything wrong in faith-professing school friends who practice homosexuality. This only logically follows the already wide acceptance of heterosexual activity among school friends anyway.

> Mama would say, "We have lost our sense of shame!"

---

1 Federal "Reserve Statistical Release, Consumer Credit," July 2010. http://www.federalreserve.gov/releases/G19/Current/

With high school pregnancy so common and celebrated, it's hard for our girls to even view it as a difficult *consequence* of sin. And some in our classes are finally arriving at the conclusion their textbook writers have hoped, "But God, God isn't really *real*, is He?"

What's happening? Is there that much disparity in teaching at home? Is it that there's too little time? These girls have a great knowledge of material things. They have strong opinions on which name brand mall store is better and why. They know what kind of car they want to drive. They even compare shopping receipts totaling hundreds. The problem is out there, and the solution eludes us, but should it? In some cases, is it as simple as giving our girls more money than sense . . . of decency?

More Money than *Sense of Compassion*

Do you know the first time the word *compassion* is used in the Bible? It's when the daughter of Pharaoh saw a little helpless baby crying in the river— she had *compassion* on him. Compassion superseded many obstacles to triumph that day. It superseded race, nationality, age, culture, economic status, family loyalty, and ultimately, the law. And it was for a baby that she didn't even know.

In the glory given to the courage of Jochebed and Miriam in our ladies' studies, the beautiful compassion of the Egyptian princess is often grossly overlooked. In a very real sense, this nameless princess fulfilled every criteria Jesus set forth for judgment of sheep and goats in Matthew 25. The little Moses was hungry and she fed him; thirsty, and at Miriam's suggestion of a Hebrew nurse, she gave him drink. He was naked and she clothed him. He was a stranger, a foreign baby she had never laid eyes on, and she took him in. He was placed alone in a basket in the bulrushes along the banks of the Nile River. If that's not imprisonment, I don't know what is. When she was compassionate toward the infant in the basket, her compassion was figuratively directed to our Lord Jesus, although she didn't know it.

Her economic status was established. Of all the Egyptian women, she had it. She had money, but the great thing is, she didn't have more money than sense . . . of compassion. Want to be like that? We've got the money part down, and for the most part, I find that women of God excel in the compassion department as well.

You can be sure that when you show compassion to a helpless individual, you show compassion to Christ. He is well able to more than compensate for your random act of kindness. You can't out give the Lord. Notice this fascinating verse in the Proverbs: "He who has pity on the poor lends to the Lord, and He will pay back what he has given." (19:17). What? Who? You mean it's possible for human us to loan money to Divine God? It happens every time we choose to help someone who could really use it. Maybe that person will return the favor; maybe not. Maybe he will come around again next month and the next. Maybe this loan will make you short on your rent money. Don't count on it. The deal is, we don't even have to sort it all out. We just have to trust the scripture and not think twice. It's a loan to the Lord. He's good for the amount—and abundantly more.

He who has pity on the poor lends to the Lord,
and He will pay back what he has given.

—Proverbs 19:17

More Compassion than Money

Let's talk about mites and Macedonians. In both cases, the widow in Luke 21 and the Christians in 2 Corinthians 8, willingly gave to a cause out of deep poverty. They had more sense than money. From our point of view, they really couldn't afford it. After the sacrifice on their part, we don't find them immediately bathing in material luxury, but neither do we find them destitute after giving their last dime (or less). Remember, God is good for the amount, and abundantly more.

Repeatedly in the New Testament we find that Christ had compassion on someone. Never, that I'm aware of, do we find Him having money. In fact, when He was required to pay taxes, He had to fetch a coin from a fish's mouth (Matthew 17:24–27). If we truly want to be like Christ, we'll have more compassion than money, and not the other way around.

In particular, Christ is described frequently as being "moved with compassion." Have you ever been moved with compassion? Perhaps a homeless person walked into the restaurant where you were eating, and ordered a single small item, the cheapest on the menu, and paid with small coins. Perhaps you've just seen a child that was enthused in play suddenly fall, and you've watched his smile turn upside down and the tears begin to drop. You're moved in a way that can't be described. That's compassion. Identify it and act upon it before the moment is gone. What can you do? Remember, Jesus said, "And whoever gives one of these little ones only a cup of cold water in the name of a disciple, assuredly,

I say to you, he shall by no means lose his reward" (Matthew 10:42). If it's just a cup of cold water that's needed, that's like a million dollars to God.

Sometimes in our rich houses and church buildings, we are so distanced from the poverty around us that we fail to be moved with compassion anymore. We listen to the voice of Satan disguised in familiar faces:

- "You can't help those who won't help themselves."

- "Haven't they read the classified ads?"

- "I've got my own family to care for."

I am in no way advocating that we give our money or the Lord's (it's all His) to a chronic liar who continuously cons churches in order to enable his sin addiction. He needs a different form of help. But we all have special families in our communities—and we know that the breadwinner has been laid off. We see people walking down the street with a dinged up grocery cart shivering in the cold. We have people among us in our worship that we know are struggling to pay the rent. When we are hesitant to help because we have to keep enough on reserve to pay the church light bill or pave the west parking lot, and we don't want to dip into the savings, we have withheld from the Lord, and we have nonverbally stated a lack of trust in His promises. He's good for the amount. Remember the proverb: If you have pity on the poor, you're lending to the Lord. Isn't the converse also true? Have we shown we have more money than sense? . . . of compassion?

More Money than *Sense of Timing*

If you've ever had a child, you know what a sense of timing is. Theirs is impeccable. It causes toddlers to run out naked in your interview with the mayor. It's in their ability to rest peacefully at night until the split second that you curl up in bed and pull the soft covers around your neck; then they open wide and cry. You dream of mommy moments in which you work puzzles together or build skyscrapers, and in which your child will beam with accomplishment as you and he share a moment looking at your creation. In reality, he shows no interest whatsoever until you have 34 dinner guests arriving in 8 minutes, and you have burned the rolls and you begin microwaving the undercooked ham in sections. He then bounds down the stairs with the entire galaxy construction set in tiny pieces and with a precious puppy expression says, "Hey Mom, want to build this with me?"

It's critical to have a good sense of timing, especially in matters of eternal consequence. Ever wonder how it is that you can see a train coming down the railroad tracks, and in a matter of minutes, you see another train going the opposite direction? Uh-oh! One set of tracks! How is this possible without a catastrophic collision? The trains are saved by one thing—timing.

Satan needs to knock only one thing off-track in our lives in order to have catastrophe, and that's our timing. If he can get the timing off-track, the rest of the train will naturally follow. And so we begin to squeeze all the things into our life that we want to do before our train heads home. We will definitely start focusing on spiritual matters when we finally get this house remodeled. The kids are too small to know the difference now anyway. There's plenty of time. We need to spend some time teaching them about life and its consequences, sin and disease, death and the hereafter. But right now the summer is short and there are so many movies, so many back-to-school sales, so many new electronic devices to try. We'll get to it just as soon as we get through this gotta-buy-right-now list. Christian camp? Christian school? Evangelism conference? That would be nice. But we do have this cruise coming up—too bad we don't have the money.

Wish we could help more. Wish we could give more to the Lord. We've got a van payment you know, but it will be paid off in three more years, and we plan to have lots of compassion then.

When you're trying to escape a fire, timing is everything. We know the rule is to escape with your own life and those you love. Don't grab the material things. Let them burn. Let them burn! *Let them burn!*

We are trying to escape an eternal fire with our own soul and the souls of those we love. We've got to let go of the material things. They're going to burn anyway. Take care of the spiritual matters first. God says He will take care of the other things for us (Matthew 6:33). In our rush to grab all the material things before the train goes home, we're destined for derailment.

Don't end up having more money than sense . . . of timing.

Not Rich Toward God

There is only one time in all of Jesus' parables that God calls a man a fool. It is the case of the accumulator. A rich man had the dilemma of where to put all his stuff. Sound familiar? He decided to add on, and God said point-blank, "You fool!" (Luke 12:20). According to the parable, that very night his soul would be taken.

A few years back, there was a great natural disaster in a large geographical area in America. Filled with compassion, a Christian agency rushed supplies to many congregations so that they might meet the needs of their communities while giving the glory to God, the true Provider. Most of the congregations acted quickly, distributing the needed items freely to those with losses. But what one church chose to do was disturbing. As a small group of about 20, they were uncertain what the future might bring, so they decided it would be most important to take care of their own needs first. Since they couldn't possibly use all the supplies immediately, they stored them in their building—just in case.

Are the things that we spend our money on real?

I think, according to Luke 12, God has a name for that. I didn't say it, but He did. The parable ends with this synopsis, "So is he that lays up treasure for himself, and is not rich toward God" (v. 21).

People walking around with invisible dogs were spending money on something that is not real. In a true sense, anything spent on material accumulation is spent on something that is not real. Oh sure, you can touch it and see it—it's tangible, it's there. But it's only temporarily real. Twice Peter says in 2 Peter 3 that even the elements will be melted. Twice he says that every material thing we know and see will be dissolved. We have all seen material things that were burned, but most of the time some shell of the item and ashes remain. Not so in the "Day of the Lord." No scientist will be able to discern even the elements that once composed mass. No periodic table. No trace. Total dissolution. Are the things that we spend our money on real? No, not for long, at least.

How is that we are so focused on something that isn't even real? At the next gathering at your home, try holding a five-dollar bill near the fire as if you are going to throw it in. Your friends and family will stop you vehemently. I guess they should. It could be used for a good cause. Isn't it interesting, though, that millions of valuable souls are dangling over an intense and eternal flame, and we are hesitant to save them if we even notice?

Could it be that we have more money than sense?

But seek first the kingdom of God and His righteousness, and all these things shall be added to you.

—Matthew 6:33

Something for YOU to Do . . .

1. Of the categories discussed, which area could stand a wake-up call in your personal life? Sense of direction, sense of decency, sense of compassion, or sense of timing?

2. What is implied by the statement, "If Satan can get the timing off track, the rest of the train will follow"?

3. What happens if we are "moved with compassion," but fail to act on that emotion?

4. Can helping someone financially ever be bad? How do you know?

5. What is fascinating about Proverbs 19:17? What is scary about it?

6. Have you ever given money to the poor without being paid back? In some way? By someone? How do you think the Lord was involved?

7. Children have a way of demanding that the priorities be right, regardless of the timing. (They don't wait to need a bottle or a band-aid.) Give an example of this in your own experience. How is it that, as adults, we sometimes postpone the urgent for the more convenient? Give an example or two.

8. How do we have constant opportunities to apply Matthew 10:42? Do we ever miss them?

9. Spend two minutes making a list of the most expensive things you own. Set fire to the list and watch it burn to ashes. This is the destiny of your material things. Resolve and pray not to let something as worthless as ashes interfere with eternal life.

10. What "indecent" traits, according to scripture, have become exalted in a materialistic society?

11. What time can you remember that seeing poverty tugged at your heartstrings, creating compassion inside?

12. What excuses do we use, and what lies does Satan tell us, to cause us to withhold our money?

13. What course of events would have been changed had the Egyptian princess not shown compassion? What course of events will unravel because you choose to show or not to show compassion in some small window of time and life?

❧ Spark Plugs ❧

And speaking of amusement parks . . .

What's so amusing? If there is a picture that we have all seen one more time than the Mona Lisa, it's the photo of the attractive young couple laughing their way down the roller coaster, blonde hair blowing in the wind. Why is it that we never see the real picture? How is it that their skin is tan and not green, that their chin(s) are not forcing an entrance into their sternum, and that their eyes are somehow pried open? How is it that from the outset they even understood how to pull that yellow foam covered tube down over their shoulders without it clicking in place two feet too early or three ribs too late? Have these picture-perfect people never waved to the summer-job-attendant-who-never-even-took-a-physics-class person and yelled, "Help me with this thing. I'm going to die over here!"

And pardon my curiosity, but who took the picture? I'm skeptical. Did it go like this? "Here, let me set my tripod up here a few hundred feet in the air on two skinny metal tubes. At just the right moment, when a giant train is coming toward me with great velocity, I'll quickly snap the photo, pack up all my equipment and jump out of the way."

Did you know that roller-coaster riding is a voluntary sport? It's true. People choose to do it. So they get in these lines on purpose and kill an hour or two sandwiched between two handrails, a sawdust filled teddy bear, and someone who must have driven from the desert in an un-airconditioned vehicle with no deodorant.

> Loose flip-flops and giant sunglasses tumble to the stagnant water below.

I always adhere strictly to the rules on these things. All arms and legs are kept within the compartment at all times, and all loose items must remain with the attendant. All food or drinks must be finished within the queue. I must be this tall to ride.

But no one else even seems to listen. That's why loose flip-flops and giant sunglasses tumble to the stagnant water below. People stick out their arms as if they are comparing fish sizes at the bass tournament. My friend Roger in high school *stood up*, if that's possible.

I, meanwhile, am composing final words to loved ones in my head and making rash promises should I live the remaining 53 seconds.

As the roller coaster came to an almost stop, Roger's head was still up high enough to graze the lattice of the loading dock. Four stitches. Roger's only concern was getting his hand stamped for reentrance after the emergency room.

Then there was that indoor one. In the dark. Shortly after take-off, the thing comes to a dead stop in midair at a height of approximately way, way up there. I'm thinking, *This is good. This is effective. If you're trying to scare me, this is working.*

"This is great, huh?" I say to my husband with feigned confidence.

There is no answer and I wonder (because it is so totally dark) if he is still there or if I just dug my claws into a stranger's thigh. Then comes the announcement: "Please remain seated," as if Houdini himself could do otherwise at this point. "We are experiencing technical difficulties with this ride, and will resume the ride when issues are solved."

Huh? What issues? Who's solving this? Can he see in the dark? How many fingers am I holding up?

Then I caught hold of myself. This is just a funny scare tactic, right? I mean this is like the swamp thing where the monster says, "Go back. Go back. Beware." Right? Right?

But it wasn't. That's just how life falls out for me. (Poor choice of words.) I'm here. I'm alive, and am just one of many who boosted the sales of eight-dollar ibuprofen through the ceiling that day.

There have been more and they have been faster and twistier and more upside-downier, and I have survived them all.

And they have yet to put my picture on the brochure. And I am still not amused.

> I am composing final words to loved ones in my head and making rash promises.

CHAPTER 9

CAN'T NEVER COULD DO ANYTHING

Empowerment

And I was afraid, and went and hid your talent in the ground.
—Matthew 25:25

There are few things I despise more than fig season. I always inwardly cheer in Mark 11 when it gets to the part about Jesus cursing the fig tree. My daddy had filled our back yard with fig trees. Why couldn't he have planted cocoa beans? I like chocolate, but figs?—I don't even like Fig Newtons. When the figs were ripe, I was but a step between misery and fig preserves. The lot fell to my sister and me to pick the figs, and I was never an enthusiastic fig-picker. It entailed climbing the tree whose branches were sticky and whose abundant leaves were incredibly itchy when even slightly brushed against. What in the world were Adam and Eve thinking?

As Mama hovered over me with the galvanized bucket, I knew it was time. "Go fill this up with figs."

"But Mama . . ." I knew I couldn't run fast enough. I couldn't say, "I don't want to." Helplessly, I whined, "But Mama, I just can't."

I had already taken the bucket because I knew I was defeated. "Can't never could," she said.

In a more talkative mood, she would say, "Can't never could do anything." Peggy's mama added, "except wet his pants."

• •

It's true. For as displeased as mamas are with "can't," God is more so. It's obvious in Matthew 25. To the five-talent man who successfully gained five more, the master said, "Well done, good and faithful servant" (v. 21). To the two-talent man who had doubled his amount, he said the same. Then we come to the one-talent man who had done absolutely nothing with his talent because he was afraid. The master's reaction was quite different, "You wicked and lazy servant."

Wicked? Do we usually think of the Christian who is afraid to teach a Bible class as wicked? How about the person who just can't go door-knocking or visit the nursing home? I thought wickedness was about serial killers, child molesters, and terrorists. It appears from this parable that it's more akin to laziness and fear of failure, even among the Master's servants.

Who Me?

Do we ever find ourselves as members of the "can't crew," just out-of-the-limelight—peripheral Christians? We may even mistake uninvolvement for humility. This kind of stagnancy may be frustrating to the 20 percent who are doing the work, but we excuse ourselves because we just *can't*.

Moses started out in "the can't" camp. He jumped from "Who me?" to "No one will listen" to "I'm not eloquent" to "I'm slow of speech" to "Please send somebody else." What did God think of this attitude? Exodus 4:14 ESV says, "the anger of the Lord was kindled against Moses." This falls right after "O Lord, please send someone else" (v. 13). At what point can I cause the Lord's anger to burn? Right at the point where, after listing all the reasons I can't, I say, "Please just get somebody else."

Gideon ascribed to the same philosophy. While Gideon was hiding in fear from the Midianites, an angel announced, "The Lord is with you, you mighty man of valor" (Judges 6:12). It sounds like God thought Gideon could, but Gideon was less than convinced: "O my Lord, how can I save Israel? Indeed my clan is the weakest in Manasseh, and I am the least in my father's house" (v. 15). These were all the credentials that God was looking for. Gideon had an excellent resume. "Surely I will be with you, and you shall defeat the Midianites as one man" was God's confident answer (v. 16).

Each Christian can, not because of his own merit, but because of God's. To say "I can't" is not an humble admission of my own shortcomings, but a voicing of reservations about God's ability. To say, for instance, as Paul did, "Neither he who plants is anything, nor he who waters, but God who gives the increase" (1 Corinthians 3:7) is not to say that I can't plant or I can't water. It is to say I can do these lesser parts because I know, beyond a shadow of a doubt, that God will do the greater part.

. . . I Can Do . . .

Little boy David knew he could because his strength was in God (1 Samuel 17). Caleb and Joshua knew they could because their strength was in God (Numbers 13). Paul knew he could when he said, "I can do all things through Christ who strengthens me" (Philippians 4:13). It is the "I can" attitude that God values in his children.

Examine more closely Philippians 4:13. Notice that the first word is "I," not "they." We are all pretty full of what "they" can do or "they" ought to do. Just who does "they" consist of? Whoever "they" is, sure has a big "to do" list! Just last week, someone called me and asked why "they" didn't have a list of speakers posted. My first response was, "Who?" I would like to meet this infamous "they," and tell her to get on the ball.

Each Christian needs to claim personal responsibility for the work of the Lord's church. I remember one lady who kept presenting the same idea for a church outreach. She rallied other members to the cause and had them also suggest it to the leadership. It seemed to be a pretty good idea, so the leaders inquired of the woman as to how she might be involved. At this point, she said, "Oh, I didn't mean me." Philippians 4:13 says, "I can do." Who me? Oh.

The second word, "can," is the crux of the message. We've examined the idea on the previous pages. Its implication is personal capability. Paul was limited at the time he wrote this verse, to be sure. His frequent reference to his chains coupled with the events of Acts which landed Paul in prison lead us to conclude that this was a prison letter. If ever there was a good time to use the excuse, "Sorry, just can't do much under these circumstances," it was now for Paul. Instead we find him saying, "I can do all things."

The word "do" is an itty-bitty word with a great big significance. There is so much work to be done. Many Christians rest comfortably in the "don'ts." One lady constantly boasted about her grandchildren, using terminology like this: "They don't smoke, they don't drink, and they don't sleep around." In our culture, there's a lot to be proud of in that. But what is that you *do*? My husband often says, if you add up a big column of zeroes, you still end up with zero. Luke begins Acts by reminding Theophilus of the things "Jesus began both to do and teach" (1:1). The horse just has to be before the cart.

Remember when Jesus washed feet? It was the only time in all of scripture that he said, "I have given you an example" (John 13:15). He wanted us to know how important it is to serve, but knowing isn't enough, according to verse 17: "If ye know these things, happy are ye if ye do them" (KJV). Want to know what true religion is? Well, it's partially about the "don'ts." James says it is to keep oneself unspotted from the world (James 1:27). That's the tagline—it's the cart, but the gist of the definition comes first: "to visit orphans and widows in their trouble."

I used to think this verse implied that if you're not one, help one! Then I examined the widows and grown-up orphans who were running circles around me in the area of service and benevolence. Even if you are one, help one!

> *Also I heard the voice of the Lord, saying:*
> *"Whom shall I send, And who will go for*
> *us?" Then I said, "Here am I! Send me."*
>
> —Isaiah 6:8

. . . All Things Through Christ . . .

Philippians 4:13 gets pretty inclusive with its next couple of words: "all things." I would like to fly, crochet a tablecloth in an hour, and oh—I have always wanted to be able to do that whistle thing with the two fingers in my mouth. Is this the promise of Philippians 4:13? We know it's not. Then what is it? As always, it's important to back up to get the context of the verse. In verse 12 Paul says, "I know how to be abased, and I know how to abound. Everywhere and in all things I have learned both to be full and to be hungry, both to abound and to suffer need." Then, "I can do all things through Christ who strengthens me." Paul was saying, no matter what the circumstances are, I can do it. Many in the church come from tough circumstances. Just last Sunday, we were discussing how we might best help one such family. Some in the discussion were obviously becoming "weary in well doing" (Galatians 6:9 KJV) when one of our ladies humbly spoke up, "We have to understand that when we offer people Christ, those people don't come to us with lives tied up in neat, pretty little packages." We were all silenced in the gravity of the simple statement. What is your package? It may be an unbelieving husband who belittles your Christianity; it may be the hardships of being a single mom; it may be literal imprisonment or that of a close family member; it may be lingering childhood scars from alcoholic or abusive parents. What is it? Whatever it is, Paul says, you can do it! Great news considering our backgrounds, right? You can do it, simply based on the rest of the verse.

"Do" is an itty-bitty word with a great big significance.

The word "through" is an integral preposition to the statement. You can bounce all around Christ with the best of intentions, but until you make that decision to go through Him, Philippians 4:13, as well as other great promises, are null and void. Christ says in John 10:9, "I am the door. If anyone enters by Me, he will be saved." Proper use of a door requires going through it. When Jesus said, "I am the way, the truth, and the life," he said, "No one comes to the Father except through Me" (John 14:6).

Chances are, as you read this, you are in the vicinity of some type of door. As you look at it, most likely you believe beyond doubt that it's a door, but that belief doesn't get you through the door. You can tell everyone within range that it's a door, but that confession has still not taken you through the door. It's possible to walk in a direction away from the door, and then to have a change of mind and direction, and begin walking toward the door. That change in direction indicates repentance, but alone, it doesn't mean you have walked through the door.

If Jesus is the door, and faith, confession and repentance are all appropriate but incomplete responses to the door, how is it then that we go through the door? Romans 6:4 gives the answer: "Therefore we were buried with Him through baptism into death, that just as Christ was raised from the dead by the glory of the Father, even so we also should walk in newness of life." To go through Christ, we do the things He did which are so connected to our being raised to a new life. If we do not go through His death, burial, and resurrection, there was really no point in His going through it. He figuratively sandblasted the entrance to heaven for us by bursting forth from the grave. That doorway is now ours. We go through Christ by death, burial, and resurrection, and all things become possible for us.

"Christ" is by far the most important word in the passage. Remove His name and there is no means to go through; there is no strength to be gained; there is nothing to be done; and "can" turns to hopeless "can't."

Finally, the fact that Christ "strengthens" us indicates that we need to keep a constant connection to Him. The world is filled with wireless communication, which I just don't get. I mean, what is going on? I can type a few lines and hit "send," and someone in another hemisphere can immediately respond in kind (or unkind). And the deal is, I'm not even plugged into anything. I'm just sitting here in the middle of plain air with a few gigabytes. Does this seem just a little weird to anybody but me? Did George Jetson even have it this good?

As Christians, we have it good. Christians have always had a wireless connection. When circumstances hit us hard, as they did Paul, we can do them because our connection remains uninterrupted. We have the greatest Server, and He supplies us with constant strength.

Wireless connections become weakened and fail when we forget to charge the PC. How reliable is your connection to Christ? He will strengthen us, but if we fail to charge with Bible reading and prayer, or we charge sporadically, we can lose bars through our own negligence. Remember your source of strength, and be the first to step up to the plate fully charged and say "I can."

Be a "Canner"

Mama's generation and the one before spent a lot of time with pressure cookers, fruit jars, and hot water sealing baths. In those days, women were canners. Summers were spent lining the shelves with sealed-up stews, vegetables and jellies—blessings stored up for a cold winter day. How many mouths were fed by the canner who put on her apron and rolled up her sleeves? She couldn't begin to estimate. The effects were never immediate, but there would be seasons of plenty in plenty of seasons because of her canning.

Those days are all but gone. Maybe a reader here and there still enjoys canning in her kitchen. If you do, toss a few Mason jars my way, as long as they're not fig preserves. But across the generations, there will always be "canners" among God's women. While we've mostly lost the art of filling the pantry with home-canned items, may we never lose the virtue of the "canner." The canner is the woman who rolls up her sleeves and says "I can." How many blessings are being stored up for a cold winter storm because today you say "I can"? When crisis hits on a cold winter tomorrow, will someone find a blessing in your work and words of yesterday? How many mouths will be fed by the little boy you spoon-fed the scriptures to with a smile, a song, and a sock puppet? The effects are never immediate, but there will be seasons of plenty in plenty of seasons because of your "canning." Philippians 4:13 says if you're a Christian, then it's automatic—you're a "canner."

After all, can't never could do anything.

Except wet his pants.

I can do all things through Christ who strengthens me.
—Philippians 4:13

Something for YOU to Do . . .

1. Look at verse 12 of Philippians 4. Paul lists a variety of his personal life experiences that he has learned to deal with through Christ. What can you add to his list? What specifically has life dealt you that you were only able to "do" because Christ strengthened you?

2. On the other hand, there are the "abound" seasons of our lives. How is it that we need Christ's strength in these times?

3. What do you view as the most important word in Philippians 4:13? Why?

4. The verse says we do all things through Christ. What other words could be substituted for Christ as a realistic reflection of where we often put our trust?

5. Are there things that are possible for some of us and not others? Back up your answer using the parable of the talents.

6. How do we differentiate between those things that we truly can't do, and those things that we simply don't want to do, or give up on before we can master? How does another maternal phrase, "You never know until you try" fit into this distinction?

7. Contemplate the statement, "When we offer people Christ, those people don't come to us with lives tied up in neat, pretty little packages." In the Gospels, what people came to Jesus with tattered packages? What tattered packages have you come across as you have offered Christ's hope to others?

8. Which is more important—the "don'ts" or the "do's"? Why? Can we have one without the other?

9. For one week, listen closely to yourself and others. Notice every time someone uses the term "they" with no particular antecedent expressed. What about "we"? Keep count of this pronoun also, when used to generalize without claiming personal responsibility.

10. Without our intending it, what things can interfere with our wireless connection to Christ's strength? What keeps us from properly charging? Where is it that we repeatedly find ourselves losing bars?

~ Spark Plugs ~

And speaking of cartoons ...

They used to be funny. Their heads used to be shaped as animal heads, you know, like sarcastic bunnies and pyromaniacal coyotes. Now they have people heads, only shaped like those in the geometry book we spent half the tenth grade trying to ignore. They tend to have the kind of disgusting facial features we spent the other half of tenth grade trying to cover up.

What happened to intelligent comedy? I find there are only two themes left in children's programming, ironically neither of which is funny. The first is audible belching which might be funny if, say, it were Katie Couric in the middle of a report on the financial crisis on the upper coast. It is generally not funny when it is geometrical-shape-head kids with only two words in their vocabulary, one of which is "BRRRRRP" and the other is "dude" so that the whole episode goes:

"Brrrrrp."

"Dude."

"Brrrrrp"

"Dude."

"Brrrrrp."

The other theme is adopting a pet which eats your couch and pulls everything out of your refrigerator and pours it on the floor. This is not funny either. This causes flashbacks to a time in my life not so very long ago, as in this morning.

What happened to quality programming? What happened to getting up early on Saturday morning because we had waited all week just to see the wittle man walk awound in ciwcles singing "Kill da wabbit!" These classics taught us meaningful lessons we would carry with us the rest of our lives. We learned that if you accidentally fall off a protruding cliff in the middle of nowhere, you can make a very cool hole in the ground the exact shape of your body. Also, if you are quickly running on your tiptoes to strategically place a stick of dynamite in another's territory, it will without fail blow-up in your hand and you will be left standing in your underwear with no hair and only three feathers. Also, if a predator is about to eat you, you must quickly put on lipstick and throw a blanket around your head and he will want to dance with you instead.

These were things which firmly grounded us. Myself? I always identified with the Pink Panther, though he was much prettier. This is because, with the best of intentions and highest of expectations, he fell victim to the saddest of outcomes, yet continued to hopelessly persevere. This is how, as a sports instructor, his student, though in traction and a body cast from the first lesson, was hooked up to a ski boat for his next. And he reminds me terribly of each part of my daily grind.

It's true. He is a part of all that I am. He is why I still enter the appliqué division at the state fair, and why I'm willing to give the discount motel at the sewer exit another chance.

Those were the good cartoons, and I say with all the dignity of the two men who argue about movies on Sunday morning right there on TV in front of everybody, new cartoons lack cartoons at all. And I haven't even mentioned the Far East genre. These don't even attempt to be funny. They're just episode upon episode about training made-up animals like Gigisquash and Parapants to do battle with one another. At least, since my kid isn't getting a good laugh, he is learning something valuable.

There is, truly, a cartoon type, which gives my boys a drive unequaled by Junior Achievement. They walk away from the set honestly believing they can jump off the refrigerator with a towel clothes-pinned to their T-shirt. And these superhero cartoons usually do teach some value about good guys and bad guys, and the inherent good-guy quality to protect. After one such good-triumphing episode, I tussled my son's wayward hair and said, "Did you learn something from that?"

"I sure did," he said. "Always make sure your cape isn't tucked into your pantyhose."

CHAPTER 10

YOU DIDN'T MEAN NOT TO

Preventive Maintenance

Test all things; hold fast what is good. Abstain from every form of evil.
—1 Thessalonians 5:21–22

The damage was done. My ear was bleeding from deep within. It was before the days of frivolous lawsuits, and dangerous toys were recommended for everyone, not just children over three. The walkie-talkies had long, metal, sharp receivers instead of rubber nubs, and consequently were ideal to stick in your sister's ear during a game of doctor in which the victim is being forced to feign an ear infection.

As the blood began to drizzle, my "doctor" threw down the weapon and shouted the four familiar words, "I didn't mean to!" The phrase was second only to "I'm telling" in our household.

Unfortunately for the defense, the parental answer was just as common. With no tolerance or sympathy for the offender, my mama would look us square in our guilty eyes and say, "You didn't mean *not* to."

• •

In the perimeters of our life, simply "not meaning to" can end in hurt feelings, spotted reputations, and taken to its full potential, even divorce, manslaughter, and a host of heartbreak. "Meaning not to" on the other hand is a purposeful preventive—erring on the side of caution if necessary to ensure that no damage is flippantly imparted. When Paul implores us to "make no provision for the flesh, to fulfill its lusts" (Romans 13:14), it's another way of putting Mama's wisdom—mean not to!

Preventive Lifestyle

How many times have you heard these words? "I never meant for it to go this far"; "I didn't mean to hurt anyone"; "You know I didn't mean it."

In contrast, how about these? "I meant for it never to go this far": "I meant not to hurt anyone": "I meant not to say it." I've never heard these phrases. Not once. And I likely never will because if a person intentionally practices caution, intentionally means not to do whatever, these words become unnecessary. We are spared pain and broken relationships with both God and man sometimes solely based on which side of the word *mean* we put the word *not*.

"Meaning not to" is a preventive lifestyle. It's looking for a way of escape up front (1 Corinthians 10:13). In the midst of the cave of temptation, there is always a hole for a beam of light. Run toward it. It's always big enough to get even my awkward frame through. But the problem is, I don't always choose to. I'm having too much fun in the cave. There's way too much to explore in here. When we avoid that window of light, a startling revelation is in store deep within the cave. We find that the beautiful stalactites are really just dirty rocks, and the glistening guano turns out to be piles and piles of bat dung.

"Meaning not to" is defensive driving, while "not meaning to" is cruise control. Imagine a driver who hops behind the wheel, puts the automobile on cruise, and doesn't turn it off from his driveway to his destination. He won't get there! Somewhere along the way of ignored caution lights, stop signs, other vehicles, pedestrians, and big livestock, there's going to be an accident or eight. Accident? Does this kind of reckless endangerment qualify as an accident? Imagine then, at the end of the scenario, the driver peeks through his broken window at the officer and says, "Sorry, I didn't mean to." Any sane driver, whether he verbalizes it or not, means not to have an accident.

Don't Hurt the One You Love

Why can't we apply the same caution to relationships, particularly those relationships which operate under our own roof? I've never won a math bee, but I know there is an unwritten mathematical equation that says our carelessness in words and tone is directly proportional to the closeness of the relationship involved. It ought to be the opposite. It's why the Mills Brothers stayed on Billboard's charts for 20 weeks in 1944 with "You Always Hurt the One You Love." It may be that the gas station attendant thinks you're the sweetest and most polite woman since June Cleaver while your husband thinks you're a stand-in for Cruella DeVil. When we walk through the door and kick off our shoes, we sometimes kick off kindness, manners, and graciousness in the process. Then we wonder why so many Christians are sitting across from a counselor repeating the words, "I never meant to . . ."

You can sometimes smell a divorce brewing, can't you? And it doesn't always smell like secret phone calls and meeting places at first. You catch it in this, "If you're trying to play a card game with her, you may as well forget it. You're going to get tired of explaining it"; or this, "I'd rather just do it myself than have to redo it when you help." And what about the eye-rolling championship? Would your family qualify for the quarter-finals? Couples take heed! Mean not to!

Ladies, men's egos are particularly fragile in this area. God made them this way so they could feel the drive to both provide and protect. It's obvious from the time sword battles begin with mop handles and coat hangers in our playrooms. There is a built-in need to overcome. When wives belittle husbands, there is a deep-seated, unseen crisis going on. Twice that I recall, my husband has commented that certain couples in our close circle were headed for trouble. I didn't get it. They were involved in the work of the church, involved in the activities of their kids, financially secure, morally astute—where's the trouble? "I just never hear her say anything good about him," my husband explained, "I don't think she appreciates him very much." My inside reaction was, *No big deal.* But it was a big deal. Both marriages dissolved in an ugly divorce

"Meaning not to" is defensive driving. "Not meaning to" is cruise control.

court. The reason my husband could see it and I couldn't is because he is a man who understands the need for appreciation. "Be kindly affectioned to one another with brotherly love" (Romans 12:10) is so relevant. It's not just about how you treat widows and visitors; it's about how you treat your soul-mate.

Careless driving at home can lead to another level of destruction. If "meaning not to" was not applied at the first level, it is imperative here. This warning is for everyone. Mean not to have an affair. Mean not to have a relationship that could have the remotest possibility of leading to an affair. Mean not to be in a building or room alone with the other gender whether at work, a social context, a counseling session, or in any other setting, including but not limited to everywhere! If you ever once think, "I hope I get to see him today" or "I hope he is there," start purposefully avoiding that person. Mean not to!

Most extramarital affairs end with "I didn't mean to," but few begin with "I mean not to."

Get the Lysol

Meaning not to is tiresome and consuming. Meaning not to let your children go to hell, for instance, can be a demanding task. It involves monitoring the TV and entertainment choices, making time for daily devotionals and praying with your children, making excruciating yet memorable choices about foregoing recreational or academic activities which are scheduled in conflict with spiritual ones, rote Bible memorization coupled with in-depth discussion and application, physical discipline, and parental sacrifice.

Look at each item in the list above. You can get through parenting without implementing one single objective mentioned, and millions of parents are doing just that. Many of these parents are bringing their kids to church on Sundays and most Wednesdays. Unlike those abusive and neglectful parents in the media, these parents would never mean to harm their children. It's not good enough in the face of the enemy; you have to mean not to with all your might.

When someone in the family comes down with a virus, the rest of us mean not to catch it. We walk around the house with Lysol in one hand and Germex in the other. We hide our personal hand-drying towels so no one else can use them. We spray down everything with disinfectant including the cat. Our skin randomly falls off in huge flakes from being washed so often, and we only have one rule—nobody breathe! No one wants a viral germ entering his digestive track.

How long does a virus usually last? Think about it; we call it a 24-hour virus. We're up and back to life's hysteria in no time. But what about our souls?

Can't we use a degree of the same paranoia? "The wages of sin is death" (Romans 6:23). The consequences are eternal. Hell is not a popular topic, but it is a real place. It has become a joke, an obsolete idea where only cartoon characters visit. No one seems afraid of it anymore. It's okay to fear hell; in fact, it's crucial. God's repetitive warnings are red flags of love. A virus? It's misery you can live through and leave behind.

Do Not Touch

Hell is misery of a different color. Avoid it at all cost. Cut off your hand, your foot, and pluck out your eye if you have to. That's Jesus' advice, for it is better than being cast into hell fire (Mark 9:43, 45, 47) where the worm doesn't die and the fire isn't quenched (vv. 44, 46, 48). Cutting off a limb is an extreme case of meaning not to, but it is Divine advice.

Has anyone ever taken a child into an antiques store without saying, "Now don't touch anything," and then giving the child a reminder every two to three minutes? This is a working definition of meaning not to. It is constantly making sure that no damage is going to be carelessly done. Otherwise, without the reminders, we know we stand a great chance of broken glass, sad eyes looking up, a frustrated antiques dealer, and an empty wallet with nothing in return, all coupled with the words, "I didn't mean to."

Don't touch. Don't get close to. Don't even look at for very long. How could God strike Uzzah down for his natural reaction to the teetering ark of the covenant? (2 Samuel 6:6–7). I'm sure he didn't mean to. He didn't mean not to! He was already in violation of the careful procedure God had put in place for the moving of this holy furniture (I Chronicles 15:15). Did David really mean to commit adultery, impregnate a soldier's wife, commit murder, lose his baby to death, and have three other sons die in due time? He didn't mean not to. He looked; he got close to; he touched. David, Uzzah, and countless others forgot to put the reminders in place.

Reminders. They are all over the place in our society. On the coffee table, in the nightstand, on the bookshelf, on the back dashboard—the Bible gives us constant reminders to avoid broken lives and eternal punishment. Beware; do not be deceived; take heed. These are all God's way of saying, "Mean not to!" Go without the reminders, and you're sure to be His child looking up with sad eyes saying, "I didn't mean to." Aforethought beats afterthought every time.

Of all the things you mean not to do, mainly mean not to have to say, "I didn't mean to."

Be sober, be vigilant; because your adversary the devil walks about like a roaring lion, seeking whom he may devour.

—I Peter 5:8

Something for <u>YOU</u> to Do . . .

1. Uzzah and David are listed as examples of those who didn't mean to, but also didn't mean not to. Think of other biblical examples. In each case, decide where in his/her life the person avoided the window of escape. Where would "meaning not to" have changed the outcome?

2. Why are we kinder to strangers than to those in our own families?

3. Have you been present in a public setting where phrases like the ones in this chapter were said: "If you're trying to play cards with her, forget it!" or "I'd rather do it myself than have his help!"? What is your outside reaction? What is your inside reaction? What do you think these kinds of comments really communicate?

4. If you are married, make a concentrated effort, for one week, to abstain from even lighthearted criticism of your spouse. Instead, try the following:

    ❀ Verbalize appreciation for one thing every day.

    ❀ Pray for him every day.

    ❀ Tell him at least once this week that you thank God for him.

    If you are unmarried, try this on an under-appreciated family member or friend in your close circle.

5. How important is "meaning not to" let your children go to hell? Think of specific resolves that you want to implement in your home for each item below. Write down a simple plan to get started.

   ❀ Monitoring the TV

   ❀ Daily devotional

   ❀ Putting spiritual activities before recreational/academic activities

   ❀ Bible memorization

❧ Spark Plugs ❧

And speaking of walkie-talkies and phones and such • • •

One time, we used to have this totally black thing that had this coily wire that was really fun to wrap around all the appliances. Attached to the coil was a humongous telephone receiver that you had to hold, if that's possible, to your ear and talk to your grandmother. This obtrusive gadget was actually attached with a long non-coily cord to the wall, as in, if you weren't home (within 20 feet of your wall), you couldn't talk. You just couldn't clip it to your belt and drive off. It just wasn't practical. It would give you saddle sores if you tried.

The thing is, it had numbers and letters on it, but no one knew what the letters were for. Now we do. It was trying to tell us that we could spell things out to our friends like CBOTWTDG and BTW,IHCP, and then the person on the other end would say, "Oh, she's trying to tell me that she's going to stop and get a cheeseburger on the way to the dog groomer and by the way, she hates chopped pickles or either she has chicken pox." It's called texting, but to do it back then, we would have had to stay in one place, give our index finger a work out, and then the person on the other end would still have no idea what we were saying because, as unfathomable as it may seem, these phones had no screen.

Now it's A3.

As unfathom-able as it may seem, these phones had no screen.

We were ahead of the times. We imagined that with the way technology was advancing—so fast that our home was now equipped with an automatic stapler saving us so much more time than the old way which was a grueling fraction of a second—there soon would be video phones. But we thought it would just mean you couldn't answer the phone unless you were fully dressed. We didn't know that on these phones, you wouldn't really talk at all.

Instead, you get to play games with digital snakes chasing you. You can take pictures of thunderstorms right when they happen and then send them to local news channels. But mostly these phones are used to vote. No, not in a presidential election or anything like that, but for more important things like who had more talent—the yodeler or the speed-eater?

And somehow, in this crazy tech-race, how is it that we have reverted? How is it that we have come full circle back to typing? How is it that those who know their capital letters, but in no particular order, are deemed ahead of those that can actually carry on a two way audible conversation in real time through the airways?

It happened like this to me recently. The person on the other end of the phone said, "Did you get my text message?"

"Yes, and I responded to it."

"No, I sent you another one."

"Oh, I didn't get it."

"Look in your inbox. It should be there."

"Hmm. I don't see it."

"I'll resend it."

"*Wait!*—Don't hang up! I know this sounds crazy, but you could actually tell me what you wanted to say, you know, like with your mouth. I know it seems archaic, but—"

Too late.

At church, after the closing prayer, we used to gather in the foyer and admire babies, but now it's phones.

"Oh, look at this one. Isn't it cute? How old is it?"

"What does it do?"

I gave such a lame answer one time, "You talk on it. It's a phone."

Everyone laughed at my wit, then went back to comparing.

"Can't you send a fax with it, or cook with it, or do your nails with it or anything?"

I decided to send a text.

".02—UR ALL HOPELESS."

I thought I was clever, you know with the two cents worth, and UR. Get it? You are?

Then I got a conglomeration back that looked like this ^^^*(: & T Now what? Is this moving forward? Cave drawings? What next? Ugga, ugga?

I hope it's a phase. Like the CB craze of the late '70s. Then, too, we could have picked up the phone a lot easier and called our friends, but it was much cooler to know the lingo.

"Breaker, breaker, 1-9, this is Coldy Moldy, what's your handle? 10-4."

It doesn't really bother me that I didn't know what "lol" was for four years. I'm secure in my ability to open my address book, to scroll down through my pictures, and occasionally to set my alarm right on those cold mornings when—Okay, okay, I know . . .

2MI again.

Top: Johnnia, age 11.

Middle: Johnnia holding son John, 1958.

Bottom: Johnnia holding Sami.
Standing in front: John Holder,
Cindy Holder, 1963.

CHAPTER 11

You Can Look All Day Where It's Not

Looking for Love and Happiness in All the Wrong Places

They should seek God, in the hope that they might feel their way toward him and find him. Yet he is actually not far from each one of us.

—Acts 17:27 ESV

We paid for the whole week on Monday. We got a lunch card in exchange, and we knew we had to have it when we went through the line, so the lady in the shower cap could punch it. Lunch was, of course, the most important subject of the day, so the paper card was a very valuable asset. If we lost it, we were told, we'd be hungry. I did.

Terrified at the thought of missing out on cardboard pizza and chocolate pudding, I searched frantically—sort of. While an intelligent place to look would be in my schoolbooks or pants pockets, it was more fascinating to look in the Barbie case and the Lego bin. "Find that lunch card?" Mama's voice came from the hall.

"Not yet." She was interrupting Barbie's costume change in the Lego trailer. I anticipated her next words because I had heard them so many times before.

"You can look all day where it's not."

• •

It turns out, most people are doing just that. It turns out, Mama, that you can look a lifetime where it's not. There is an ongoing search for fulfillment, meaning, purpose, happiness. These concepts are more tangible than we might think. They are not fugitives hiding in impossible places. Proverbs 1:20 gives the image of wisdom calling out in the town square, a pretty obvious scene. Verse 24 says, "I have stretched out my hand and no one regarded." Could it be that this wisdom is the fulfillment, meaning, purpose, and happiness at large? Proverbs 8 presents the same image of wisdom loudly beckoning from a prominent place. Verse 11 says, "For wisdom is better than rubies, and all the things one may desire cannot be compared with her."

The "Know" or the "Know-How"?

What is it that you desire? What would really make you happy? Let's say the next time you open a Diet Coke, a genie pops out. What would you ask for? Hold that thought. Now let me guess what it's not. It's not wisdom; am I right? I've asked a lot of people what they would wish for in the genie scenario, and I've gotten some great answers. One lady told me she would wish for all the foods she loved like cheese and Oreos to have no calories. The Bible has a list of wishes that are no good. It's called "all the things one may desire." Now go back to what you wished for. Wouldn't it fit somewhere on this list? It's an all-inclusive list; *all* the things one may desire. Whatever is on your list cannot be compared with wisdom. It's not that it pales in comparison. It's not that on a scale of one to ten, your heart's desire is a one and this is a ten. It's that they cannot even be compared. They are not even on the same scale.

And yet this wisdom is screaming in the open square. It's conspicuous; I believe we can find it. Over and over in Proverbs we are told the value of wisdom, but I wonder if we really get it. I hear scholars debate over the meaning of wisdom. Some say it's the application of knowledge; others say it's not "the know" but the "know-how." Most think it's a culmination of education and life experiences resulting in an informed outlook.

These are pitches all around the batter's box which never cross the plate. These definitions leave most of us thinking that it must be really nice to be wise, but since we haven't arrived yet, we'll be at the tanning bed waiting. Deep down in your childhood Bible memory work, you know what wisdom really is, don't you? "The fear of the Lord, that is wisdom, and to depart from evil is understanding" (Job 28:28).

Fulfillment, meaning, purpose, happiness are in one place—the Lord, and "you can look all day where it's not."

It's Not at the Bank

Success in this society is directly measured with a dollar sign. When we say she is successful, we are generally talking about what sits in her driveway or the label on her purse. As Christians, we know these do not reflect true success, but the dollar drive in our world is so powerful that even *we* lose focus. I'm amazed that at the last two funerals I attended, both eulogies included what kind of car the person had acquired.

If money equals success then Judas lived a full life. I don't know the exact equivalent of thirty pieces of silver in our currency. I know that many have said it was a paltry amount considering it was the price of betrayal. But I do know this: It was enough to buy a sizeable piece of real estate (Matthew 27:7). Add to this the amount he had already embezzled (John 12:6), and he was on his way to material success.

> "The fear of the Lord, that is wisdom."
>
> —Job 28:28

The "happiness" he experienced as a result is graphic: "Then he threw down the pieces of silver in the temple and departed, and went and hanged himself . . . and falling headlong, he burst open in the middle and all his entrails gushed out" (Matthew 27:5; Acts 1:18).

While Judas' infamous end is unique in that it was a critical component in the Story of Stories, his demise is much too commonplace. How many superstars can you name who have accumulated millions, only to take their own lives in helpless desperation? How many more materially wealthy people have never made the national headlines but have had the same miserable end?

A lady moved into my neighborhood one Wednesday—the nicest house on the block. When I went to welcome her, I learned that she had just paid cash for the house. She walked me around the just-delivered furniture, an amazing collection of huge and elaborate European antiques. Her dilemma was that it was not all going to fit in this fairly large house. I remember thinking, *It must be nice.* We talked on several occasions, she attended church with me once, but she repeatedly expressed a sense of emptiness. After moving 250 miles away from her, I received a phone call from a friend. My neighbor had been found dead in her elaborate home from an apparently intentional overdose.

It was haunting to remember my thought: *It must be nice.* My neighbor was looking for something to fill the void in her life, and she would have been the first to tell you, "It's not at the bank."

Her story was more complex than we will ever fully know, and I'm sure the same can be said of Judas's. Material gain can be a tremendous blessing when used as such; it can expand the cause of Christ. However, it is never the source of fulfillment. Judas held a bag of money that was needed to sustain the Lord and His disciples in their ongoing ministry. It became, instead, an impetus for betrayal.

Your Moneybag

What's in your moneybag? As a disciple, it is there to sustain you and yours as you endeavor to further the cause of Christ. Be careful; it can easily become the very impetus for betrayal. Our money, a financial blessing from God, can be the thing that Satan uses to snare us. And we let him do it while we stand with one foot in the church door and a Bible on our coffee table.

There are two sides to every coin in the bag. There is the side that enables us to afford lots of activity. What kind? It takes money to go to plays and movies that ridicule religion. It takes money to buy backless formals and dance event tickets. It takes money to engage in tournaments which take precedence over scheduled church assemblies. It takes money to go to the beach and wear what you would not wear to the mailbox while you skip Sunday and Wednesday nights. It takes money to buy a social drink or two. That's the spending side of the coin.

Then there's the "hold tight" side of the coin. We want to make sure we have enough for a rainy day even though we'd like to help a missionary, even though we'd like to send our daughter to a Christian college, even though we'd like to put more in the collection plate. After all, there is really a need for a bigger barn right now (Luke 12:18), or van or house or fill-in-the-blank.

Judas honored Jesus with his lips. What more honorable lip service is there than the kiss? But while his lips were saying one thing, his heart was saying another. His monetary priorities had disabled his heart. In Mark 7:6, Jesus amens Isaiah's earlier prophesy: "These people honor me with their lips, but their heart is far from me." What people? Who me?

When monetary priorities disable the heart, it is no longer Judas who is betraying the Friend and Savior.

If you're looking for meaning and purpose at the bank, let me introduce you to Solomon. He was what we call "filthy rich," making himself more of a Fortune 5 than 500. See 1 Kings 10 for an amazing description of his material success. All of his drinking cups were made of gold, for instance, because silver was counted as nothing (v. 21). It must be nice, right? Careful! This is what he had to say about it, "He who loves silver will not be satisfied with silver; nor he who loves abundance, with increase. This also is vanity" (Ecclesiastes 5:10).

Some trust in chariots, and some in horses; But we
will remember the name of the Lord our God.

—Psalm 20:7

It's Not at the Salon

If there is anything that our society places more emphasis on than money, it's surely physical beauty. It's phenomenal. Almost without exception, the first two words said when a baby is born are, "She's beautiful." That baby then spends the rest of her life trying to live up to this standard.

While teen boys and some men spend a moderate amount of attention on their own physical looks, admit it—it's the women who really fall victim to the beauty trap. We are the ones fluttering from diet to diet to get the figure right. We are the ones coloring the hair. We pluck the eyebrows, paint the eyelids, outline the lips, do the leg lifts, try to zip our jeans—do some more leg lifts, and try to zip our jeans again. You almost never see a man stand in front of a mirror, change angles two or three times, and say, "Does this make me look fat?" How many times do you check the mirror every day? It's more than you think.

We stay in this uphill battle only to ultimately lose because society determines our value by the way we look, and we contribute to the lie. We mean well when we constantly tell children how pretty they are. We almost cannot help it because we grew up in this same world. It is ingrained in us that beauty is important. How much better would it be for the children if we commented on how kind they were, how helpful, or how good?

I have already referred to this as a battle we will lose. You know as well as I do that we cannot look like the model on the magazine cover. She is technologically enhanced. But even if we can achieve Hollywood runway looks—and some of you will come closer than others of us—how long will that last? What will that model look like in twenty years?

I'm amazed at the lengths we will go to in trying to maintain youthful looks. Recently, *My Beautiful Mommy* was featured as "the perfect Mother's Day gift" on a morning show. The book, written for young children, is about a mommy who gets a tummy tuck, breast implants, and a nose job. The mother explains, "You see, as I got older, my body stretched and I couldn't fit into my clothes anymore. Dr. Michael is going to help fix that and make me feel better." She tells the child that her nose will soon be "different, my dear—prettier!"[1] This, in my estimation, is an exploitation of the innocent. It has never occurred to any four year olds that his mommy isn't pretty because her breasts are too small, her tummy too large, or her nose too imperfect. Mommies are beautiful because they kiss boo-boos and make smiley faces out of mustard. They are beautiful at three in the morning on the bedside of a feverish child, though at that moment, they have probably never physically looked worse.

The Passing or the Praising

Can the tummy tuck really make you feel better as the mommy in the book says? That's what the world is looking for, isn't it? Where is the fulfillment? If it's not in the hairstyle, it must be in the new outfit. If it's not in the outfit, it must be in the suntan. If it's not in the tan, it must be in the nose job, until the

---

1 Michael Salzhauer, M.D., *My Beautiful Mommy* (Savannah: Big Tent Books, 2008).

desperate search on the beauty aisle gets more and more extreme with multiple piercings and exotic tattoos because it seems there is nothing else left.

"Charm is deceitful and beauty is passing, but a woman who fears the Lord, she shall be praised" (Proverbs 31:30). Here they are side by side in one verse, beauty and the fear of the Lord. Is it just coincidence that these two are contrasted? What are we pursuing, the passing or the praising?

To assign value to a person based on outward beauty, even if it is self, is to devalue our Lord Jesus Christ. Isaiah 53:2 says he has no form or comeliness and there is no beauty in Him. As He hanged on the cross to free me from my guilt, He was about as physically grotesque as we can imagine. And yet there was a beauty here beyond any physical beauty which has ever existed or ever will. We are assured, "Neither is there salvation in any other" (Acts 4:12 kjv), but we can continue looking all day where it's not.

It's Not on the Ladder

Set a ladder in the middle of the back yard where children are playing, and suddenly, no toy on the property has appeal. Every child is going to abandon what he is doing, and try to climb to the top. It's a built-in drive that we have from the beginning, the desire to climb. It's how cookie jars get broken, and sometimes lives and homes.

The futile attempt to find happiness through climbing is something hundreds of thousands are buying into. It begins in kindergarten if not before. Every mom's child is the best reader. Good grades are more important than anything else. People without a college education are viewed as second-class. There is a separation of class between colors of collars. When you take a survey for a marketing team, they inevitably want to know your highest degree of education.

There is nothing wrong with ladders. They help us hang light bulbs and reach storage boxes, but few decorators will design the entire scheme around the ladder. There is nothing wrong with being a good reader. In fact, it's vital to obedience to God that you are able to know His will. Good grades are signs of discipline and increased knowledge. A college education can equip a person to serve in specialized areas, and to provide for his family (1 Timothy 5:8). There is nothing wrong with advancing in a career. In fact, Christians should stand out in the workplace because of the guiding principles of integrity, self-control, character, and relationship skills inherent in the scriptures.

Notice, though, with the ladder in the backyard, no child gets up there and stays. There are too many important things going on around it. There are too many important people in the yard.

The Lasting Ladder

There is no lasting or real fulfillment in ladder-climbing. It can keep you from the good activities and people around you. There is only one ladder you can climb which has no top, and that is the ladder to heaven. I recommend it because it keeps you only from those things which will hurt you spiritually, and it's a ladder you can climb together with your children.

If you think happiness, contentment, and self-worth can be found on career and education ladders, you need to be introduced to Bertie Mae. Bertie Mae was too busy picking cotton to get a formal education as a child, but she was one of the wisest ladies I have ever met. She feared the Lord. She lived in a rusty trailer out in the country. It was very clean, but I remember seeing a field mouse run across the floor on occasion because of the open cracks. Bertie Mae didn't know about career ladders, but she had quite an education in God's Word. There was contentment in this little trailer that was better than rubies. It was a place of laughter and family, and so the guests came in to fill their glass with sweet tea and wisdom. If you couldn't find an open chair, you could hop on the side of the bed in the den. She didn't succumb to Martha Stewart. She continued to climb the real ladder that matters, and it led her straight where she knew it would.

Why is it that so many of the wealthy, the educated, and those at the top of the ladder need therapists and sleeping pills? Could it be that this is another dead end road in the search for fulfillment?

Let's go back to our teacher Solomon. Here's what he said of his own career success. "There was no end of all the people over whom he was made king" (Ecclesiastes 4:16). Sounds like the top rung to me. Read on: "Yet those who come afterward will not rejoice in him. Surely this also is vanity and grasping for the wind."

> *Then Haman told them of his great riches, the multitude of his children, everything in which the king had promoted him, and how he had advanced him above the officials and servants of the king.*
>
> —Esther 5:11

So Where Is It?

Millions of people are looking for that missing piece to make their lives complete. Solomon had cleaned out every corner where most people are searching, and over and over again in Ecclesiastes, he announced, "It's not here."

A radio station broadcast that it would host a city-wide treasure hunt. The winner would receive five thousand dollars. Each day on the air, the DJ gave another clue to the mystery. The proximity became clearer, and there was a certain part of town where hundreds of people began to mill. They were wading in park fountains and removing manhole covers and lowering themselves into sewers. Some were even crossing into high voltage caution areas.

Meanwhile, in the adjacent library, a man oblivious to the search, picked up a book off the shelf. After thumbing through a few pages, he placed it on the table and laid his head on it for a needed nap. When naptime was over, he raised his head and spotted the corner of an envelope sticking out from the book. Half-heartedly, he examined the outside of the envelope, shrugged, and then stuck it back in the book. Before leaving, mild curiosity caused him to give the envelope another look, and this time he opened it. As you've guessed, it was the claim ticket to the five grand.

> All that time . . . the answer was in the book.

All that time, it was in the book. All the frantic searching, endangerment, lost work time, ruined clothes, and exhaustion spelled futility for the treasure seekers. All that time, it never occurred to any of them that the answer was in the book.

Is that a parallel or what? People are searching for the fulfillment they so desperately need in their lives. Where is the missing piece? "I can't get no satisfaction 'cause I try and I try and I try and I try," screamed the Stones in the sixties.[1] And millions are continuing to try and try again, but they are all coming up with empty buckets because they are looking in all the wrong places.

At the end of Solomon's desperate search, he found the claim ticket, and he opted to share it with the rest of us to save us the trouble of searching. Is your life incomplete? Would you like to be whole? Here it is in the closing words of

---

1 Mick Jagger and Keith Richards, "(I can't get no) Satisfaction," *Out of Our Heads*, 1965, 45-LON 9766 (USA).

Ecclesiastes: "Fear God, and keep his commandments for this is the whole duty of man" (12:13 KJV). "Duty" is a word supplied by the translators, so the phrase really more accurately reads, "This is the whole of man."

Connect back to the thoughts at the beginning of this chapter. Anything you go after cannot even be compared to wisdom (Proverbs 8:11). Wisdom is the fear of the Lord, according to Job and other inspired men. Wisdom is calling out to us from an obvious place (Proverbs 1:20). And now the exhaustive searcher for the missing piece, Solomon, says, "This is the whole. Fear God and keep his commandments." There is only one place to find His commandments, and that is in the Book. All the searching, all the false leads, all this time . . . The answer is in the Book.

Second Corinthians 13:11 says, "Become complete. Be of good comfort, be of one mind, live in peace; and the God of love and peace will be with you." Does this kind of completeness sound like the right fit?

It's calling from a prominent place. You can have it if you like, or you can look all day where it's not.

> *Let us hear the conclusion of the whole matter: Fear God, and keep his commandments: for this is the whole duty of man.*
> —Ecclesiastes 12:13

Something for YOU to Do . . .

1. Give Ecclesiastes a quick look. Make a list of other places Solomon has explored and found futile success.

2. What is it to fear the Lord?

3. Most people holding this book are among the top one-third of the world's wealthiest. We are financially blessed. Think of specific areas where we need to be careful not to allow the blessing to become a stumbling block.

Name ways that even Christians use the thing God has blessed them with to pull them away from Him.

4. In contrast, list ways we can use financial blessings to pull us closer to Christ.

5. Another thing Mama said was that when people go on vacation, they sometimes say, "Bye, dog; bye, cat; bye, house; bye, God." List some nonverbal ways "Christians" communicate that they have left God at home while on vacation.

6. Encourage every child you encounter this week by complimenting him or her about a non-physical characteristic.

7. Why is our society so ingrained in the beauty lie? What subtle messages do we constantly soak in?

8. Do some research on the Roman beatings in New Testament times. Describe what Jesus' body must have looked like.

9. Why do you think women are so much more concerned with physical looks than men are?

10. How do you feel about elective cosmetic surgery? What other methods of attaining attractiveness are just as extreme?

11. Does society actually determine treatment of individuals by their physical looks? Do any do this in the church? Consider James 2:1–4.

12. What specific things are ladder-climbers missing out on?

13. To what degree is ladder climbing healthy? Which gender is more prone to climbing? Why?

☙ Spark ⚡ Plugs ☙

And speaking of screaming guitars . . .

What's wrong with the amp that we had? It was compact, portable, and quiet—meaning, it could be heard only from the stop sign. My son wanted bigger and better, and with his recently acquired wealth from science fair winnings, there was no stopping him.

If there's one thing that thirteen has brought him, it's focus. The boy used to leave half-eaten hotdogs on top of the basketball, and he would brush his teeth with a pencil and toothpaste. Our conversations went like this:

"Can I have a pirate ship?"

"I don't know. How much money do you have?"

"Jason has eighteen dollars?"

"Is he buying the pirate ship with you?"

"Who? What pirate ship? Is this a Happy Meal toy?"

"That's a soap dispenser."

"You should have seen him. He karate-chopped the whole thing with his left foot."

"Who?"

"Hey, can Martians really disappear if you show them a dirty sock?"

Now we're focused. There's only one subject at hand all the time. "Have you heard me play *Smoke on the Water*? Can I look up guitar tabs? Do you want to hear *Smoke on the Water*? Do you know how many watts Jason's amp is? This sounds like *Beat It*, but guess what? It's *Smoke on the Water*. Do you know how much a Fender Stratocaster costs? Can I have an amp with more watts? Can you play *Smoke on the Water*? I can."

It's not just my son. It's everyone else's son, too, who comes to my home to see if Abram's amp really can be heard in Morgan County. They can all play *Smoke on the Water*, too. Twice. Each. Every night.

I wonder if they'll ever get past the twelfth note. Anything is possible, right?

And it's this whole thing with guitar video games. What happened to the fat little ball that went through the maze eating dots including the one dot that made it invincible? Now that was a sensible video game. What happened to shooting aliens and double-jump squashing gorillas?

Move over, junior. Now you're messing with your mama's game.

What is it with these crazy kids, actually trying to play some musical instrument hooked up to a computer screen, and then yelling, "Whoa, I'm 139th in the world! I'm so awesome."

It doesn't help that part of the fun is laughing at the old rock artists that we were once—face it—scared of. We were just a little uneasy to think that the person on our album cover who painted stars around his eyes and had a black, tapered tongue might really exist and be coming to an auditorium near us. I can't remember many controversies bigger than when a member of the youth group actually wore a "Guns N' Roses" tee shirt to the skating rink. It was "in your face" to the establishment when two great guitarists who could only spell "Z Z" grew beards to their navels.

Now it's just a big joke, right? A vintage costume party. HA HA.

Well, move over, junior. Now you're messing with your mama's game. Give me that thing. My boyfriend once taught me *Smoke on the Water*, too. My solo is interrupted.

"Look, Mom! You're 14,321st in the world. You're ranked! You're right next to Qui Mu Souis. Can you grow a beard to your navel?"

Anything is possible, right?

Top: Baby John supported by Johnnia, 1958.

Middle: Lee, Johnnia, and John Holder, 1958.

Bottom: Johnnia sterilizing baby bottles, 1963.

CHAPTER 12

BECAUSE I SAID SO

Accepting God's Authority

There is a way that seems right to a man,
But its end is the way of death.

—Proverbs 16:25

They had no idea of the magnitude of the risk to their very lives. Dozens of motorists were humming along the Birmingham roads as if it were any other ordinary day. But this was the day that my 15-year-old sister acquired her permit. The state government actually permitted my sister to operate a car, as in a big thing with four wheels and an engine, on an actual road that had innocent people on it. This was the same person who only last year had received a bicycle for Christmas, and on a trial run, having no idea what handbrakes were on a steep downward asphalt incline, jumped a ditch and did a half-flip before crashing and sending seven Christmas packages flying into the nearby picnic table and an unknowing dog.

The fact that I was along for the ride in this first automobile-operating venture probably has something to do with my complete boredom with *The Dukes of Hazard*. I remember near brushes with mailboxes and jogging shorts, but mostly I remember my mama's abrupt directions. (The same government which permitted my sister to drive also required a parent or legal guardian to ride in the front seat. This is unfair to mothers who, after 15 years, have already been spit up on, pushed out of the bed, and held hostage at unending awards ceremonies.) "Stop" she announced in C-sharp, followed by another "Stop" which contained all the chords of my *Introduction to Harmonica* book.

The one word in between those two "Stops" was priceless: "Why?"

"Because I said so!"

Isn't that always the answer? I know that there are some pretty high-paid professionals out there who tell us not to use this philosophy, and there is probably some merit to their advice. Curious young minds can learn from the logic behind directions. It can also break a child's spirit or build resentment when there is never a chance for the child to explain his perspective, but she is always met with an "I said so, and that's the end of it" decree.

These allowances excepted, "Because I said so" is a sufficient reason for obedience in and of itself. There is not always time for a logical discourse when your child is stepping into traffic or climbing a guardrail. Ephesians 6:1 does not give a guide for rounds of affirmative and negative dialogue, after which, if the child agrees, he should obey the parents.

> There is not always time for a logical discourse.

Open communication in which parents take the time to both listen and encourage is ideal. Allowing a child to make his own decision and experience consequences equips him with a life skill. However, there are some decisions which a child is not yet capable of making and which cannot be adequately explained to him because of his still developing cognitive ability and limited life experience. In view of this, a child should know that "because I said so" is an absolute verdict. There has to be an instilled respect for authority.

And so it is with God, only more so. Is it necessary to have an explanation of why God wants us to do the things asked of us? There are a zillion reasons why "because I said so" from Almighty God is good enough. Since I can't count to a zillion, let me list five.

Reason 1: He Is All-Caring

It seems plausible as a mother, that because I am the one who carefully carried the fetus within my womb for nine very interesting and nauseating months, because I am the one who went through birthing contractions that felt like a hyperactive porcupine had been released in my lower back in order to bring the helpless infant from a world filled with darkness into bright fluorescent light, because I am the one whose unsuspecting breasts underwent traumatic adjustments in order to satisfy the growing baby's frequent hunger, because I retrieved LEGO bricks from the toddler's mouth, because I rocked away monsters in the middle of the night—somehow it seems only fair that the same child needs only, "Because I said so."

How much more should I accept as final the authority of the God who carefully created me, who knew me before I was in the womb (Psalms 139:13), who endured the sting of thorns and the merciless blows of sharp bone-laced lashes, who in the form of His only Son, at last laid down His innocent life for me, all to bring me out of darkness into his marvelous light? (1 Peter 2:9). He keeps constant count of the hairs on my head (Matthew 10:30), He knows what I'm about to ask for before I utter a word, and His very presence dispels monsters in the night. It qualifies Him to say, "Because I said so."

Reason 2: He Is All-Knowing

My four-year-old did not know that a stove element which had just brought fudge to the soft-ball stage would burn the palm of her hand. I knew, but before I could scream the warning, the damage was done. We were the first emergency room customers for the millennium: January 1, 12:01 a.m. (We have a way of celebrating major holidays in such grand fashion.) She didn't understand the danger involved because she just didn't know. She was four, and four-year-olds can't discern between danger and safety. They are sometimes known to scream hysterically at a housefly before proceeding to stick a pair of scissors in an electrical outlet. They don't know. Children are born with a knowledge of virtually nothing at all. We, on the other hand, because we are somewhere in the neighborhood of about very-much-older, have an incredibly deeper under-standing of electricity, heat conductors, and the non-threatening anatomy of houseflies. Knowledge alone is a basis for "because I said so."

In the book of Job, the lead character (at least the human one) is stuck in the "why" zone, and he demands an answer. "But I would speak to the Almighty, and I desire to reason with God" (Job 13:3). He gets a sufficient one, but it's not quite the one he was expecting:

Now prepare yourself like a man; I will question you, and you shall answer Me. Where were you when I laid the foundations of the earth? Tell Me, if you have understanding. Who determined its measurements? Surely you know! (Job 38:3–5)

By what way is light diffused, or the east wind scattered over the earth? (Job 38:24).

Can you send out lightnings, that they may go, and say to you, "Here we are!"? (Job 38:35).

Have you given the horse strength? Have you clothed his neck with thunder? (Job 39:19).

Does the eagle mount up at your command, and make its nest on high? (Job 39:27).

Shall the one who contends with the Almighty correct Him? He who rebukes God, let him answer it (Job 40:2).

We are not in a position to ask God why, because our knowledge is way too limited to understand His greatness. It's like we are four. His all-knowing wis-dom is so far beyond our grasp that we must accept His "because I said so" with full confidence in Him as Maker, Sustainer, and flawless Director of our lives.

If you are not particularly tech-savvy, suppose your computer is misbehav-ing one morning, which probably doesn't take a lot of imagination for any of us. You call the customer service line, and after experiencing several birthdays, you talk to a knowledgeable person in the service field who begins asking questions and giving directions: Click run, type in msconfig, open this window, check this box, uncheck this box. As he talks you through a diagnosis and solution to your problem, imagine if after every direction, you ask why before obeying. Can you imagine the frustration of the technician who has a working knowl-edge of the computer, with the constant questioning of someone who has little understanding of a mouse cord? It seems it would quickly get to the point of, "Ma'am, this is the company that made the computer! Do it because I said so." We generally are glad to follow the instructions of a complete stranger because we understand that his knowledge in that field will greatly help us who have very little knowledge. Shouldn't the infinite and ultimate knowledge of God Almighty receive greater respect than that of a certified computer technician?

Reason 3: He Is All-Seeing

Yes, this means that He sees the cheat sheet in spelling class that the teacher doesn't see. He sees the Oreo you devour but do not count. But it means so much more than that. He sees the consequences of your actions before you can perform them. He truly is ahead of the curve. When Satan's offerings look promising and attractive, we can easily be fooled by the decorative exterior of a putrid and destructive package. But God is not fooled! He sees the personal pain and despair that this sin package will bring to His own child. Because He sees, He says, "Thou shalt not," and because He sees, He says "Thou shalt," which is just as important.

It's why we are commanded to assemble every Lord's day. It's why we are to be in submission to our husbands. It's why we are to study, to pray, to teach, to esteem others better than ourselves, to give, to help, to live peaceably, to be thankful, to do everything without complaining, and on and on the rules go for Christian living. Why? Because He said so, and because He can see the exact benefits, and how these benefits are going to unfold in my personal future.

The third-base coach tells the seven-year-old on second base, "Don't worry about being safe or out. Just do whatever I tell you. If I say run, don't hesitate. If I say stay, don't move." The child can then obey with no fear of the consequences. Whatever happens, he knows he did the right thing just by trusting and obeying the coach, who by the way, has a much better perspective on the whole field. He can see it all.

If we put this much confidence in a human baseball coach, how much more should we entrust our spiritual game-plan to an all-seeing God?

For this is the love of God, that we keep His commandments. And His commandments are not burdensome.

—I John 5:3

Reason 4: He Is All-Able

Sometimes in the great big consumer world, we feel we are unfairly treated, so we get on the phone to see if we can work out this difference between how a company should treat a customer and what actually transpired. The first words of the phone call are usually, "How can I help you today?" and often that person can't help us at all. That's when we say, "Can I speak to your superior?" We keep going up the telephone escalator until we reach the corporate lid. Sometimes this person will make a good effort to amend any dissatisfaction for the benefit of the company. Other times, we hear the frustrating words, "I'm sorry, I can't help you."

Those are words that God will never say. He has no superior. When we bring our needy souls before His throne, we have reached the Top. This is the God who parted the Red Sea, who made the sun to stand still, who coded each strand of DNA thousands of years before anyone else had heard of it. He was the manna God, providing some 87 billion meals if you do the math, just in the wilderness of Sin. Is His provision today really any less impressive?

Among those who crossed that sea and ate the manna, there weren't a whole lot of detailed explanations behind the behaviors commanded and expected of them. We don't find the Israelites asking if it would just be okay to paint blood on one of the doorposts rather than on both sides and the top since that would save time and materials and would be less dangerous. It would, after all, show compliance with the idea. They didn't try to reason with God about gathering manna on the Sabbath. They simply obeyed or disobeyed. Many learned lessons along the way. Some of the names were Nadab, Abihu, Aaron, Korah, Dathan, and Abiram. The primary lesson was, "Because I said so."

Reason 5: He Is God Almighty

God is. It's the only answer I need. From a fiery bush that would not be consumed, from ground too holy for Moses' shoes, God directed Moses to go and stand before Pharaoh to deliver His people. Moses tried exemption from every angle, until finally he asked what he would say when the people asked who sent him. "And God said to Moses, 'I AM WHO I AM.' And He said, 'Thus you shall say to the children of Israel, 'I AM has sent me to you'" (Exodus 3:14).

God says 162 times in the Old Testament, "I am the Lord":

- *You shall keep My Sabbaths, and reverence My sanctuary*: I am the Lord (Leviticus 26:2).

- *Therefore you shall keep my commandments, and perform them*: I am the Lord (Leviticus 22:31).

- *Nor shall you profane the name of your God*: I am the Lord (Leviticus 19:12).

Almost every command concerning worship, speech, eating, sexual relations, and treatment of the poor, handicapped, strangers, and servants was confirmed with the phrase, "I am the Lord."

It was profoundly conveyed: "Because I said so."

Not "Because I Think So"

There are a number of commands which don't make sense to us as children of God. Really, can sin be washed away by being dunked in water? Well, that's what He said: "Arise, and be baptized, and wash away thy sins" (Acts 22:16 KJV). Since it's a figure anyway, does it really matter how it's done or if it's done at all? How can eating unleavened bread and drinking grape juice make communion with the Lord? Well, that's what He said,

> The cup of blessing which we bless, is it not the communion of the blood of Christ? The bread which we break, is it not the communion of the body of Christ? (1 Corinthians 10:16).

We begin to reason that, since this is also a figure, it might be more meaningful if we approached it from a human perspective. Why not once a month, once a quarter, on holidays, or some special weeknight service rather than each Lord's day?

Changing gears, would God really fault a couple who wanted to get married, though their first marriage was dissolved just because of incompatibility? Well, that's what He said,

> And I say to you, whoever divorces his wife, except for sexual immorality, and marries another, commits adultery; and whoever marries her who is divorced commits adultery (Matthew 19:9).

We can rationalize a lot of things which may make sense to us, but we are not all-seeing, we are not all-knowing, we are not all-capable, and we are not the Almighty. He is God and we are man, and "the way of man is not in himself; it is not in man who walks to direct his own steps" (Jeremiah 10:23). It has never been about "because I think so."

The Bible opens with "In the beginning . . ." By the third verse, we have the full premise for our being and behavior: "And God said . . ." That expression is used six more times in the creation chapter, "And God said" is followed by "and it was so." From the very beginning, it has always been, and it always will be "because He said so."

Then God said, "Let there be light"; and there was light.

—Genesis 1:3

Something for YOU to Do . . .

1. Remember the last time you were pulled over by a policeman. Recount what he said and what you said. Suppose you had asked him why the law was made, why he must enforce the law, why you have to obey the law, or why you have to pay the ticket. What kind of scenario would develop from this?

2. Which of the above questions do you think we present to God? In what ways?

3. Contrast 2 Samuel 24:14 to Hebrews 10:31. How do these verses reconcile? Considering both of them, whose authority would you rather be under, a human policeman or the Divine God? How are these sometimes one and the same?

4. What particular thing does God require or expect of you or someone else, which may have sometimes caused you to wonder, Why?

5. Make a list of the people you are unable to approach because of their authority and your lack of it. What could each provide for you if you were able to approach him? What on this list is a parallel to what God provides? How do God's authority, approachability, and provision work together?

∽ Spark Plugs ∾

And speaking of birthing . . .

When did people start scalping tickets for this? I want my friends and neighbors to look at the little bundle through the glass. I felt bad enough for the doctor to have to see me like this, and I sure wouldn't want anyone to see me who would actually ever recognize me again in Wal-Mart or anything, not to mention my own in-laws. I have friends who invite them all, dragging in lawn chairs and popcorn for the big event.

> I felt bad enough for the doctor to see me like this.

I've never performed it before a live audience, but I have been through the experience several times. I use the word *experience* to mean that moment in life when you have the pristine feeling that you are being run over by a rotary tiller at the exact moment your finger is being slammed in a car door while a dentist who predates local anesthesia is giving you a makeover.

I've run through the gamut of medical professionals, too. My first was Mary Jane. She was a sergeant of a birther who had been doing this a hundred and twenty years. She was on duty alongside Dr. Someone-Who-I-Won't-Say-His-Name. The deal with this clinic I was using was that you could visit any doctor you liked during the nine-month holding period. But then, when you actually went into labor, you had absolutely no choice about who was on duty.

All my friends loved their birthing doctors. "I hope you get Dr. Smith," they would say, "But Dr. Johnson is really wonderful, too. Only, whatever happens, I just hope you never, ever get Dr. Someone-Who-I-Won't-Say-His-Name."

I kept up with everyone's shift. I was planning to have one of those labors where you just finish knitting a baby sweater, look at your husband and say, "I think it's time. But wait—first, let me look to see if Dr. Someone-Who-I-Won't-Say-His-Name is on duty."

It didn't work like that at all. I was about to consume a scrumptious southern supper at my in-laws when my water broke, and I helplessly looked at my husband and said, "I think it's time."

And he said, "What? The nursery is covered with a tarp. The wall is half painted. I'm out of spackling compound. How long do you have after your water breaks? Can you wait until next Tuesday?"

I got to the maternity floor and said, "I think my water broke."

They looked at me, and said, "Yeah. It broke."

"So who's on duty?" I said with my fingers crossed behind my back.

"Dr. Someone-Who-I-Won't-Say-His-Name."

"Oh."

It was quite okay, though. About that part, at least. I usually have a different take on people, and I really liked him. Besides, you rarely see the doctors in these cases anyway. That's where Mary Jane comes in. She gave orders like a crossing guard on awards day. All night, she told me when to push, how to push, and a list of all the people who didn't push right.

"Squeeze your husband's hand," she barked.

He lovingly replied, "Aaaaoooowwwww-Aaaah!"

It was nothing a couple of weeks in a splint wouldn't cure.

And then when my beautiful son finally emerged into the world, Mary Jane announced—I'm not kidding—"It's a banana head."

Oh that all of my nurses could have been as experienced as Mary Jane.

With my second baby, I piddled around the house all day, thinking, "Hmmm. If I didn't know better, I'd think I was about to have a baby. Silly me. Everyone knows no one is actually born on her due date. Ha-ha."

By the time my husband comes home, I'm saying, "Do (bend over) *you* (massive groans) know how many (laying on the floor now) babies are born on their due date—Aaaaooowwww-Aaah!"

To which he replied, "Did someone just squeeze your hand?"

This time it was December, and when we got to the maternity floor, they honestly said, "No room at the inn."

And I said, "Where's that epidural thing?"

When I was quite insistent on staying, they put me in a regular room because there were no more delivery rooms. They must have handled the shortage of staff with a temp service because they hooked me up to a lot of stuff, gave me a powerful enema dosage, and then the nurse said, "Wait. How are you going to go to the bathroom hooked up to all this? Just lay here and let me go ask my manager. I'll be back."

Mary Jane announced, "It's a banana head."

What? Wait? Lay here? I took the law into my own hands and dragged the equipment with me which just might have had something to do with the fact that the monitor was not reading correctly.

My contractions were showing up like little pimples occasionally appearing on a serene line on the screen, but they felt like the Alamo.

"I want my epidural!" I said with the politeness of a serial killer in heroin withdrawal.

I was patted. "Oh, there's plenty of time for that," the temp said, smiling at the peaceful screen.

"What are you, crazy? Something's wrong with that aaaaooowww-aaah!"

"Did someone just squeeze your hand?" my husband said.

She adjusted the monitor which now looked like the stripe on Charlie Brown's tee-shirt, only taller. She checked me.

"You're about to have a baby."

"Not without an epidural, I'm not!"

This is when—this is true—they wrapped a blood pressure cuff around the I.V. that is for some reason mandatory before you can get an epidural, and were pumping the cuff to squeeze that fluid into me as quickly as they could, while I yelled, "Hurry!"

Now that I was experienced in when and how to push, they repeated only one phrase, "*Don't push!*"

One of the nurses recognized my husband from a funeral she had attended. "Hey Scotty," she yelled, "Catch!" She threw him a couple of tubes. "Here. Grab that box. I'll get these. Now get that end of the bed. You push and I'll pull. We've got to get her to a delivery room."

And he's saying, "I'm paying you how much to work for you?"

The doctor on duty delivered nine babies in the next few hours. On his routine rounds the next morning, he came and plopped on the edge of my bed.

"How you feeling?" I said to him, and patted his knee.

"Well, Celine, I want you to know that . . ."

But I never did. His voice trailed off, and he never even finished that sentence, but I had a beautiful baby girl, and that's all that mattered. I told him to get some rest, and sent him on his way.

Only the fourth baby was induced, due to my distance from the hospital and the fact that I was strep-B positive. By now, I'm giving the orders. The nurse came in to take my blood pressure and listen to the baby's heart.

"You need to start an I.V." I said, "It's important for the antibiotic to circulate before the baby reaches the birth canal."

She agreed and said she would tell the other nurse.

The second nurse came in to give me the drug to induce labor. "But I need an I.V. first," I said. "It's important to—"

"That's right," she said, "We need to take care of that."

Pretty soon, the doctor strolled in with a big smile. "How we doin'?" He patted my foot.

"Good, but don't I need an I.V? I'm strep-B positive, remember? And I need an antibiotic."

"What?" He addressed me sternly, "You're supposed to tell us that kind of thing before now."

You're supposed to tell us that kind of thing before now.

I felt like such a lousy patient, letting the whole medical staff down that way. I really should have given them more advanced training of the protocol for this scenario.

I had the baby. He was as beautiful as the first three, but there was more of him to love. He was whopping, having already completed most of spring training.

"Too bad we induced," my husband said, using the infamous "we" word. "I would have liked to have seen how big he would have gotten if we had let him come on his own."

"How's your hand?" I said.

"It'll be okay in a couple of weeks with a good splint."

Celine and
her fourth child
Enoch, 2002.

Top: Left to right: Mattianne, Enoch, Abram, Celine, and Miriam Sparks, 2002.

Middle: Left to right: Abram, Enoch, Scotty, Mattianne, and Miriam Sparks, 2010.

Bottom: Left to right: Mattianne, Celine, Enoch, Scotty, Miriam, and Abram Sparks, 2004.

CHAPTER 13

DON'T GO HUNTING WITHOUT YOUR GUN!

Consistent Bible Study

Your word is a lamp to my feet, and a light to my path.
—Psalm 119:105

Mama did many things well. She could make a doll out of a hair-spray bottle and an earring during a long trip in the car. She could make teacakes that put Mr. Keebler and his little elves to shame. Though she was practically blind without her glasses, those eyes in the back of her head couldn't have been keener. But of all the things Mama could do outside of mothering itself, it was pretty undisputed that she could teach a fifth and sixth grade Bible class best of all. No one wanted to get promoted out of her class. The terror of the bus program who climbed out of windows and broke crayons in all the other classes sat spellbound in hers and did all of his outside work. People from all walks of life attended her funeral, many having but one thing in common—they had once been in the fifth and sixth grade.

There were no shiny bulletin boards or glittery stars in Mama's classroom, but it didn't take long to know what her Bible class was all about—it was about the Bible. Inevitably, after each promotion, someone would come in one Wednesday frazzled and late trying to slip into an empty seat while Mama was talking, but she would stop mid-sentence: "Carl Jeffrey Jones, where is your Bible?"

"I forgot it."

"Well, you've come hunting without your gun!"

Any sixth grade boy in that part of Alabama could see the uselessness of a hunting trip without a gun. He got the point, and from that day on, he brought the Bible.

• •

Do we have the same insight that Mama gave that sixth grade boy? There is a certain futility to our lives simply because we are out hunting without our gun.

Not My People

Hosea 4:6 says, "My people are destroyed for a lack of knowledge." The destruction was not due at first to some blatant sinful act, but the root cause is merely a lack of knowledge. The chapter opens with a rebuke for no truth, no mercy, and no knowledge. What naturally follows in the next verse is a horrific unfolding of the result: swearing, lying, killing, stealing, and committing adultery. Notice this is not about people in general, but specifically *My* people. It's entirely possible for us, the people of God, to reach the same place of depravity through simple negligence of reading the Bible. Are we going to get Bible knowledge anywhere else?

In 2 Kings 23 we find King Josiah tearing down idols, trying to restore decency to the nation of Israel. Though Josiah's intentions were noble, he was leading a nation of people who had gone hunting without their gun. The book of the law of God had been misplaced. It's probably more accurate to say it had been ignored. When found, it was found in the temple of God, a logical place if anyone was looking. When Shaphan the scribe read the book before Josiah, Josiah tore his clothes, a custom to show extreme despair.

Even a king who had at his heart service to God and destruction of idols was so far off course without God's book to instruct him that, with this one reading, he knew his nation was incurring God's wrath for its vast disobedience. No matter how good our intentions are, if we neglect to read God's word, our actions are going to be way off course. "It is not in man who walks to direct his own steps" (Jeremiah 10:23).

Josiah simply did not know. I truly believe that there are generations who simply do not know. The television has said that it is right and good to have a range of sexual experiences outside of marriage. The textbooks have said that humans have evolved over millions of years from lower life forms. The movies have said that those who believe that there even is a right or wrong value system are narrow-minded and that religion is a hate-based entity—a direct contrast to James's definition. All this has occurred while the Bible has lain on the coffee table mostly unopened and undisturbed.

Take Your Vaccine

In Acts 17:11, the Bereans were praised for their studying the scriptures daily. Can we get by with less? Maybe, if that's all we're trying to do. Can you get by with eating less than every day? Probably, for a time, but you'll become very weak. We expect God to give us this day our daily bread. This day. Just this day. How would it be if, in response to our physical need, God skipped days sporadically and tried to load it all upon us in one day to make up for those missed meals in the past? We couldn't survive very long with this kind of inconsistency.

How can we expect to survive spiritually with the same degree of inconsistent feeding and nurturing? Peter compares us to newborn babes who need the milk of the word to grow (1 Peter 2:2). Do babies skip feedings because there are too many other demands at the time?

Sadly, we lose sheep from the flocks of our churches from time to time. The loss of even one is too many (Luke 15:4). They used to be here. Where are they now? There are a number of complicated circumstances unique to each member of the Lord's church. Discouragement rears its head, sin waits

> Josiah was leading people who had gone hunting without their guns.

at the door, adversity thickens the plot, relationships may be too weak, and materialism tugs at the sleeve. Whatever the list of causes, the dropout has lost all. She's not a number on the board but a soul at large, out of range of the Father's protection. And while the Father undoubtedly bids her come back, and we her family hopefully magnify the sentiment, unless she repents she is headed for eternal damnation.

Could she be you? I know she could be me. How do we keep the assurance that we will not drift to this point? I really believe that daily intake of God's scriptures, guidelines for living, encouragement for adversity, strength for temptation, and faith for the doubts—if these are constantly instilled in us through our own reading—will struggle with any power that tries to pull us away. I'm not about judging others, and I have definitely fallen short in Bible reading myself, but I just wonder if there has ever been one person who just sort of dropped out of church attendance and fell away while she was actively reading her Bible every single day. It's a vaccine! Take it.

But that's difficult to do, isn't it? It is so hard to get that one-on-one time with the Lord in because Satan knows it's the vaccine. He means to make it hard for us. He means to talk us into waiting until tomorrow when things will hopefully slow down a little and we won't be as tired.

Daily Dose

The things that are keeping us from reading the Bible are good things. We're nursing babies and preparing meals and visiting the sick and kissing boo-boos and reading bedtime stories. What of this do we want to eliminate? None of it. That's why we've got to stop and eat spiritually, just as we do physically, in order that we might continue to do all these things effectively.

*And when He had opened the book, He found
the place where it was written.*

—Luke 4:17

Resolve: No Matter What

So where's the solution? It first lies in resolve. There are so many things in life that we just have to make a decision about. We have to say, "Okay, this is it. From now on, this is what I'm going to do and I'm not going to skip it *no matter what.*" That's what gets us to church on crazy and hectic Sunday mornings. We made up our mind years ago that we weren't going to skip. Imagine, if instead, we had said, "I'm going to try to go to church when nothing else hinders me."

Discipline

Another solution to the spiritual feeding problem lies in discipline. Have you ever got up to brush your teeth when you were too tired to move? You did it because of discipline. You didn't want to, but you knew that overnight decay would occur if you didn't remove the plaque on your teeth.

Am I suggesting that there is a time we should read the Bible when we don't want to? It's possible. Didn't you ever try a vegetable for the first time when you didn't want to? Think of all the times you've benefited from and enjoyed that vegetable since. Why? All because you were disciplined enough to do what you didn't want to do at first. If we're not disciplined enough to make ourselves read the Bible when we're tired or busy, it really is like the toothbrush. Decay will build up in our lives and create problems that could have been avoided with a little preventive maintenance. Getting up to read the Bible when you don't want to is like laughing in Satan's face. He thought he had you.

> Reading the Bible when you don't want to is like laughing in Satan's face!

Support

Notice, with the Bereans, "they" searched the scriptures daily (Acts 17:11). It wasn't one person; it was a group thing. Alcoholics and other addicts recover through accountability. It's necessary to their wellbeing for another person to know how they're doing. There's nothing wrong with asking in a Bible class, "Who has read your Bible every day?" Some do it with a show of hands, some mark it in a record book, and some turn in a checked-off list. This is in no way bragging about alms or deeds. Rather, it's a way to look out for each other, to keep each other accountable. It's loving one another enough to care if we're all being fed.

It's extremely helpful to have a reading friend. This can be a person in your household like your husband or daughter, but it doesn't have to be. If you're both reading the same chapter each day separately, you cross paths at some point during the day or week and make observations about it. I know people who actually fill in Bible workbooks and then meet weekly to go over them. While this is great, you can read "together" in much simpler ways. Discuss it over coffee, over the phone, or easiest of all, send a quick email. It might be just a couple of sentences about how one particular verse stood out.

> *So Philip ran to him . . . and said, "Do you*
> *understand what you are reading?" . . . And he*
> *asked Philip to come up and sit with him.*
>
> —Acts 8:30–31

Creativity

You may have to create a time to read your Bible. Get a purse-size Bible and a magnifying glass if you need it. There are lots of moments in the day that you didn't know you had. Do you eat lunch alone? Do you wait on the bus? Do you wait on the doctor? Do you sit in the car waiting for a child at ball practice or music lessons? If all else fails, I'll bet you drive somewhere. Get the Bible on CD.

Getting creative to find Bible-reading times just might serve a dual purpose. You can be sure that—while you're not doing it for this reason—if you're quietly reading your Bible in a somewhat public place, someone is going to notice. Someone will eventually say something which should inevitably lead to your inviting him to worship God or study with you.

The Whole Armor

Mama wasn't really the first to use the gun illustration. Paul had done it about a couple of thousand years earlier in Ephesians 6. Well, he used the gun of that day which was the sword. In his illustration, there was a lot of other necessary gear the soldier should be concerned about: righteousness, truth, peace, faith, salvation. Can you imagine, though, this well-armed soldier arriving in the heat of battle fully armed? He's practically invincible, except for one thing—he forgot his sword! He can stand protected for some time. I'm sure with his armor he is better off than the man with none. But there is nothing to ward off the attacker. Doom is inevitable.

As Christians, we have received the truth and made the decision to live a life of righteousness. Through faith we have obeyed God which brought about salvation through His grace. This has resulted in an all-encompassing peace. We're fully armed. This armor, as invaluable as it is, can work only when it is used in conjunction with the sword, "which is the Word of God" (Ephesians

6:17). There's a warfare going on for your soul (Ephesians 6:12). Don't go out there without your sword.

Don't go hunting without your gun.

And take the helmet of salvation, and the sword
of the Spirit, which is the word of God.

—Ephesians 6:17

Something for <u>YOU</u> to Do . . .

1. Research hunger fasting and learn what happens to the human body in each phase. What parallels can you draw about spiritual fasting?

2. What do you think causes dropout in the Lord's church? Which might be countered by daily Bible reading?

3. For one week, keep a Bible in the same room with the television. Each time you hear the TV say something that contradicts truth, set an item on top of that Bible. Note how long it takes for the Bible to be "lost" in other things.

4. Count the number of items on the Bible from the previous exercise. How many more times did the TV teach something in your home than the Bible? Which needs to lessen and which need to increase? How can you go about getting this in balance?

5. Read 2 Kings 18:6. Could it be that this book was in full use at this time? How is it that it could be completely lost and forgotten by the time of Josiah? How can we help ensure that this does not happen for our grandchildren?

6. To what degree does Bible reading affect our eternal destination?

7. What are some sources aside from the Bible that give us biblical instruction? What are the benefits of these? What are the dangers?

ᨆ Spark Plugs ᨆ

And speaking of hunting and ball practice . . .

I never intended to be a soccer mom. That's something for someone with 2.5 kids and a minivan. I've never cared much for the social norm. I didn't wear a cap and gown at graduation, I vowed I'd never buy Tupperware, and my cell phone doesn't slide. But after I got to 2.5 kids, I began to wear down. I found myself drinking cappuccino and wondering who was voted off the island. I rationalized that soccer was a form of fencing, and believed my mini-van to be an extended Beetle.

We had played soccer before. And of course, when I say we played soccer, I mean we sat on the bleachers and ate cheese curls and said, "Who's winning?" But that was before we moved to the Delta. Where we came from, the girls and boys played together and the only thing that really mattered was if we were going to get a discount at the pizza party and who was paying for the trophies.

We moved to Cleveland, Mississippi, on a Saturday, and the deadline to sign up for soccer was Monday, so we signed up without thinking it through. In this town, the girls play at one park and the boys at an entirely different park on the complete opposite side of town. Someone planned this on purpose to confuse my life and has probably planted hidden cameras all along College Street which runs the distance so they can have a good laugh every evening in the playback. The first day of practice I took my son to what I hoped was his park. I thought no one was there and I must be in the wrong park, but come to find out, everyone was just sitting in their vans protecting themselves from the strong Delta February wind. I think this is a good strategy which has not proved to win us many soccer games, but has seen a significant drop in the number of ear infections.

Anyway, when I found out I was in the right park, I proceeded to rush my daughter to the other end of College Street. Here, there were a lot of squaws sitting on the bleachers wrapped in blankets, and there were clusters of little girls. Scattered hither and yon was a man or two. Each had blue lips, cracked hands, and an expression of helplessness which said to me, "No one read the Soccer Coach Clause to me before I signed the Fatherhood contract."

My little girl and I ran from cluster to cluster saying, "Is this the Diamonds? Is this the Diamonds? Are we on the right field? Are you my mother? Who's paying for the trophies?" By the time she found the right team, the other moms had forfeited to Mother Nature and were sitting in their vans, heaters running, cell phones attached.

I left my daughter, to go pick up my son. In the meantime, I passed my husband, who was trying to find out who was at what park, three times. We kept turning around at the bank and crossing paths. It's called figure driving and would make an excellent winter sport. I think the Cleveland Park Commission should consider it because you can play it in February and your lips don't change colors.

> Moms were sitting in their vans, heaters running, cell phones attached.

By the time he got to my son—he lost the coin toss at the four-way stop—my son had told the coach he wasn't practicing in this weather and the two of them went home. This led to Mom lecture 342, the one about staying committed to something once you start, but I knew in my heart he was right.

So anyway, there. We had reached the place in life where the boys and girls were now separated in organized—and I use the term loosely—sports. And this is where you learn the real difference between boys and girls. It's not about hormone levels or fire trucks and baby dolls. The real difference in boys and girls is what goes on at soccer games. At the boys' games, the coaches all have hemorrhoids so they never sit down. They are convinced the boys are losing the game on purpose, and so they are incensed and yell at the top of their lungs that they are going to write their own children out of their will if they let the ball get by them again. Moms, slip a sedative in your husband's coffee. We will all sleep better.

> The real difference in boys and girls is what goes on at soccer games.

At the girls' games, the parents sit in their blankets and say,

"What's the score?"

"I don't know, but fall merchandise is 60 percent off. You better hurry. Go blue!" (We say "blue" because we can't even remember the team name.) "Speaking of blue, I got a blueberry candle and it matches the washcloths. Kick it, Megan! Did you know there are zero fat grams in a Lifesaver? What's the score?"

So at half time, we ask the girls what the score is, but they don't answer because they have a mouthful of Hershey bar because it's all about snacks, and the parents are secretly praying that the whistle will be blown to start the second half so we can devour what's left of the bar.

When the game is over, we suddenly remember why all the people with nice cars are the people with no children. Before we moved to Cleveland, we thought Mississippi mud was a dessert, not a sport. And so the post-game ceremony of stripping down your children and putting them in garbage bags before buckling them in would begin. You think we could save ourselves some time and just smear the mud directly all over our kids and skip the games?

Skip the games? When are they anyway? It went like this: The game which was rained out last Tuesday will be Monday after next before the game rained out today. The game which will be rained out tomorrow was played yesterday provided there was no rain.

Call me a radical, but I'm just thinking out loud. I'm wondering if it would make sense to anyone else to play soccer in maybe, say, the fall. I'm just thinking the parents might actually get out of their vans and the kids would think someone was watching them besides the coaches with hemorrhoids. I'm just wondering if it might be more fun if you didn't have to chase the goal which is being blown into the lake.

Or is this just a case of paternal revenge? Did this really start in the mind of a Delta duck hunter who was standing in water at five a.m. with ice forming on his waders? Was it then that he remembered his children back home sleeping in a heated bedroom? Was that where the concept of winter soccer was formed? "Just wait!" I imagine he whispered as he formulated the plan. "When duck season's over, you're going to be running around in a field of cold mud, wind blowing your shin guards off, and I'm going to be in a heated minivan drinking sedative-laced coffee."

Holder Family, 1972.
Standing: John, Cindy, Sami
Seated: Lee, Johnnia, Celine.

Johnnia with
grandchildren Caleb
and Hannah, 1990.

Lee Holder and a Christmas Chihuahua, 1956.
Johnnia bought "Cheetah" (the mother) and "Doo Dad" (the puppy)
for her husband for Christmas. She had to keep the dogs quiet in the house
all night Christmas Eve (and it was a tiny house). She was the queen of surprises.

A Life Filled with Christ and Common Sense

Johnnia Duncan Holder
1929—1992

Celine's mama, who coined or borrowed the phrases which make up the chapter titles, was born on June 6, 1929, to John and Mattie Duncan. She was the fourth of five children, the only girl, and was named Johnnia. The Duncans were converted to Christ one by one, through the teaching of Joe Hyde, the local preacher in the small town of Jacksonville, Alabama.

As a child, Johnnia worked for a while at the "picture show" on the square. At 16 she finished high school and enrolled at Jacksonville State Teacher's College, where she acquired her teaching degree. While still single and into her early marriage, she taught school in the Calhoun County communities of Blue Mountain and Coldwater where it seems they didn't even know the Depression had ended. She told stories of barefoot children and still others who scavenged the dump to find clothing and shoes. She began every day in the public school by reading the children a Bible story.

In 1953, Johnnia married Lee Holder, and they had four children—the last, Celine, born in 1964. Through the years, Celine remembers grown men calling their home to talk to their fourth grade teacher once again.

Johnnia died at age 63 from cancer, and some time after that, one of those Blue Mountain students found Lee's residence, searching for his teacher. He had recently become a Christian, baptized into the Lord's church.

He just wanted her to know.